The Hypocrite

Ron Winter

©2020
SPECTRE COMMUNICATIONS
ALL RIGHTS RESERVED

THE HYPOCRITE
Copyright ©2013, ©2020 by Ron Winter
Cover Design by Valerie Connelly

All rights reserved. Printed in the United States of America. No part of this book may be reproduced or transmitted in any form or by any means, electronic or mechanical, including photocopying, recording, or by any information storage and retrieval system without written permission from the publisher, except for the inclusion of brief quotations in articles and reviews.

This is a work of fiction. Names, characters, places and incidents either are the product of the author's imagination or are used fictitiously and any resemblance to actual persons living or dead, business establishments, events, or locales is entirely coincidental. The publisher does not have control over and does not have any responsibility for author or third-party websites or their content.

If you purchased this book without a cover, you should be aware that this book is stolen property. It was reported as "unsold and destroyed" to the publisher, and neither the author nor the publisher has received any payment for this "stripped book."

For information about Spectre Communications please
visit RonaldWinterBooks.com
Email: RWinterBooks@comcast.net

Library of Congress Cataloging-in-Publication Data

Winter, Ron,
THE HYPOCRITE / Ron Winter
ISBN 13: 978-1-7348369-1-2
Murder Mystery

May 2020

9 8 7 6 5 4 3 2 1
Printed in the USA

The Hypocrite

★ ★ ★

Prologue

Smythe – The Colonial

*A man who moralizes is usually a hypocrite,
and a woman who moralizes is invariably plain.*
—Oscar Wilde (1854-1900)

Moran Smythe watched with trepidation as the red ant crawled up his arm, waiting for the bite that was sure to come when it found something interesting. It stopped several times to explore the beads of sweat on Smythe's forearm, then kept moving, always forward, yet taking whatever time it wanted to explore side to side. It reached the sore that had been bothering Smythe for the past several days, ever since a barb pricked his arm as he ran through a blackberry patch down by the river. In the sore the ant found the perfect spot.

"Damn!" Smythe exploded. "Damn!"

"Master Smythe, there will be no more of that!" His warden, a dour-faced Pilgrim with no sense of humor and even less patience with anything that smacked of blasphemy, admonished the blasphemer.

"Damn this ant, and damn you, too!" Smythe shot back, his patience long since evaporated in the heat. It was late June. The laser-like sun overhead focused on Smythe, as though he were a mere ant trapped under a lens. Smythe—dirty, unshaven, smelling of sour

The Hypocrite

sweat, whiskey and body fluids, his head throbbing, his stomach burning, and his mouth feeling as though it were stuffed with dry cotton did not need a lecture from the prig who was assigned to watch him while the village elders decided his fate.

In Windsor, Connecticut, in the year 1646, those who did not pull their weight or show proper reverence for the Almighty met with swift rejection. Connecticut, still decades away from becoming a chartered colony, obeyed The Fundamental Orders of 1639 which governed the affairs of the community by requiring a combination of thrift and strong belief in God. Moran Smythe hated work and showed reverence for neither man nor deity.

"Your attitude has not improved with the new day, I see," the warden replied. "Continuing on your present course will only serve to extend your stay in the stocks."

A reply boiled inside him, but Smythe hesitated, heeding the warning. A group of exasperated villagers forced him into the stocks sometime the previous evening when his confinement began. Smythe was drunk and out of control when they swarmed over him, dragging him to the village green to confine his arms and legs in the pillory. Now, at midday, here he still sat, his hangover adding to his overall misery.

In the meetinghouse adjacent to the green, the elders were discussing Smythe's actions of the previous evening and the desirability of his continuing on as a member of the community. Their moods, bereft of sympathy, matched Smythe's anger, Some even preferred that he stay in the stocks until only a skeleton remained, un-Christian as that fate might be.

"That shall be it then," the leader, Elder Clarke, declared as the discussions ended. He stood tall, in his thirties, ruddy and wiry then strode toward the meetinghouse door, the remainder of the group of a

The Hypocrite

dozen or so following in his wake. They exited the building and made straight for the green and the stocks.

"Here comes the decision now," the warden remarked to Smythe. "If I were a wagering man I'd bet you aren't long for this area."

Smythe glowered but decided against answering, holding out the briefest of hopes that the elders wouldn't expel him.

That hope vanished when he saw the look on the Elder Clarke's face. The elder wasted no time on pleasantries.

"Master Smythe, it is the decision of this council that your actions can no longer be tolerated, and you are hereby banished from the community of Windsor—forever!"

"But Reverend," Smythe protested, deliberately giving Clarke a promotion in his religious standing that didn't fool Clarke for an instant. Nonetheless, realizing the unpleasantness of his fate, Smythe finally succeeded in rousing himself enough to plead for a lesser punishment. "I know I had a bit too much of the devil's brew, but it hardly warrants banishing me!"

"That's enough," Clarke retorted. "It isn't just your drinking. It's your disgusting behavior, your filth, your rudeness, and your continual refusal to make even a token contribution to the welfare of this community. We have had enough of you."

"But I've made a contribution," Smythe blustered. "Just the other day I brought in enough blackberries from the patch by the river to make pies for the entire outpost. Why look, I still bear the scar on my arm from the brambles. And I may have been a bit under the weather last night, but banishment? It seems excessive to me."

"Referring to the Reverend Williams' wife as an overstuffed whore of Satan hardly qualifies as being under the weather, Master Smythe," another of the group retorted.

"That is quite enough," Clarke interjected, obviously not pleased

The Hypocrite

with reliving the events of the previous evening in public. "We will tolerate no more discussion and you are hereby banished."

With that the warden stepped forward and released Smythe from confinement. Smythe took a moment to let the circulation return to his limbs, and then finally stood erect. He, too, was tall, about six feet, and once lean and promising. But the years of drink, slothfulness, and sheer selfishness took their toll. His belly now protruded over his belt and his once full head of hair was quickly receding, turning from gray to white.

A perpetual scowl lined his face. He wore dirty clothes, not just on the previous evening, but as a matter of course, and he reeked—so much so that the elders stepped back as one when he rose from the stocks, not out of fear, but to put as much distance between Smythe and themselves as possible to ward off the stench.

"But where shall I go, brother?" Smythe pleaded.

"To the north and west are Indian tribes," Clarke responded. "To the east are Boston and the English, if you can make it there unscathed. To the south are the Dutch. The choice is yours."

With that, another elder spoke up. "You could even try the settlement of Wethersfield," he suggested with a sly smile. "Why, I hear they even built themselves a tavern. Just the kind of community that would make your kind feel welcome," he said.

Smythe glared at the group, which seemed to be involved in a private joke, their faces in various stages of smiling, just short of outright laughter. His musket, powder and shot were dropped on the green before him, along with a deerskin bag holding his meager belongings. He gathered them up, took one last look, and declared "I'll see the lot of you in Hell."

The elders gasped in concert, but before anyone could react Smythe turned and strode off, heading south. "Good riddance," one

The Hypocrite

remarked as they turned toward the meetinghouse to resume the business of the day. Within minutes Smythe was out of sight, and the community of Windsor quickly forgot that he was ever among them.

 Smythe made his way south without delay, figuring he could cover the dozen or so miles to the Wethersfield settlement before nightfall. On this June day nine hours of light remained, all nine of which could be put to good use if he didn't dally.

 He chose a path along the Connecticut River that would take him to the settlement at Hartford, but where he had no intention of stopping. They knew him there, in a similar fashion to the way he was known in Windsor, and there would be no welcome waiting for him.

 Wethersfield thrived as a trade center, populated with recent arrivals who had no experience dealing with Smythe and his less than desirable personal traits. He hoped to avoid meeting any of the Indians who also inhabited this part of the New World. More than a few braves figured he owed them more than he paid when dealing with them.

 Smythe made his way along well-worn game and Indian paths, heading steadily south. The physical activity alleviated the misery that still lingered from the previous evening's excesses. In a few hours he circumvented Hartford, returning to the Connecticut River trails well south of the settlement.

 Emerging at the edge of the village of Wethersfield, Smythe could see the sun dipping toward the horizon in the west. He smelled the smoke from cooking fires a mile away, and before arriving at the edge of the clearing, scouted out a reasonable camp site. Smythe had no idea who he would meet in Wethersfield, nor how he would be received, and so assumed in advance that he might not have a bed that night.

 He skirted the cove where ships from England disgorged their

The Hypocrite

cargoes of goods and humanity. Once around he took a brief detour to the east toward the river. He made his way to a dock and warehouse in search of employment or lodging. Seeing no one about, Smythe headed for the center of the settlement. Several good-sized houses were scattered along the road to the cove, and now and then he could make out bits of conversation as cooking aromas wafted on the gentle twilight breezes, until the two-story building at the southern side of the community caught his attention.

Smoke curled from the center chimney, and the sounds of animated conversations spilled from the open door. In the near darkness Smythe walked up the entrance path and for a brief moment stood framed in the doorway, his eyes adjusting to the dim interior.

He entered then, to a sudden silence as all eyes watched him make his way to the bar along one wall. Tankards of English ale were in evidence, and motioning to the young woman working as barmaid he ordered one for himself.

As he sipped his ale in silence the conversation gradually returned. Smythe noticed a game of chance in progress in the far corner. No stranger to cards and dice he approached the table, appearing first to be just an observer. A player motioned to an empty chair. "Care to sit in?" the player asked. Smythe accepted. The game used dice instead of cards, commonly called the Devil's picture book by the more religious inhabitants of the village. Familiar enough with its rules, Smythe needed no instructions to play the game.

He pulled some coins from his deerskin pouch and for a time hovered between winning and losing, occasionally raking in the winnings, other times handing them over to other players. But an educated eye could see that even though he sometimes lost, he never lost as much as he won, and Smythe's winnings continued to grow.

Over time other players left the table until only Smythe and the

The Hypocrite

tavern owner, a large and boisterous drinker named Browne, also a notoriously bad gambler and an even worse loser, remained.

He did not have to do anything special, other than stay in the game and oppose Browne. Browne wagered all of his money, even collecting some from other patrons. But Smythe kept winning.

In the end, Browne lost what little composure he had and dared Smythe to go all or nothing, betting a one-half ownership in the tavern against Smythe's winnings. Less than a moment later Smythe was transformed from a banished drunk to a suddenly prosperous co-owner of the only commercial food and drink establishment in Wethersfield.

Browne raged at Smythe, who smiled grimly and announced, "Drinks on the house." Browne glared at Smythe, a vein in his temple throbbing as he clenched and unclenched his massive fists. The other patrons rushed to the bar, drinking free ale before Smythe changed his mind or Browne changed it for him. Smythe's offer bore no good will. Speaking that one brief sentence established Smythe as a true co-owner and showed his intention of exerting control over his half of the business.

Browne paced back and forth before the open fireplace. The bright flames from earlier in the evening had diminished to coals. The barmaid was banking them for the night, leaving just enough so in the morning she could restart the cooking fire without requiring much kindling.

Even the dim light of a dozen candles could not mask Browne's fury. Gradually, first one, then another, and finally all of the patrons made excuses to leave. They didn't know Smythe, but they did know Browne, and they didn't want to be called forth to provide testament to the evening's sudden change of events.

With only the barmaid present, Smythe made a public effort at reconciliation.

The Hypocrite

"Look friend," he told Browne. "I'll give you a chance to win it back in a week or two. But let me work with you for a bit and you'll see that having me as a partner isn't such a bad thing."

Browne was beside himself, refusing to even consider Smythe's offer.

"Well then, I'll see you in the morning—partner," Smythe said with emphasis, gathering his belongings and heading for the door. "I made a camp up the hill a ways to the west. I'll sleep there, and meet you back here on the morrow."

Browne, his eyes flashing with a murderous rage, snarled a reply so filled with hatred and anger that it emerged as unintelligible gibberish. Smythe didn't care. He saw and heard all he needed.

Smythe strode away to the west, quickly disappearing in the deep darkness of a colonial American night. A few lantern lights twinkled in the sitting rooms of houses along the main street of the settlement, but otherwise no one stirred. Smythe didn't go all the way to his camp, instead walking only a few hundred yards in that direction before stopping, turning and watching the path he had just navigated.

After a few minutes he determined that no one was following him. The community made no noise, not even a barking dog.

Smythe quietly returned toward the tavern. He stopped inside the tree line but at the edge where the brush gave him good cover for watching the building's front door. He could see better at night than most, and even though there was only starlight and a very pale sliver of a moon, Smythe could make out all the necessary details.

After a half-hour or so the barmaid left the front door and headed down the main street toward one of the houses. Smythe noted her leaving, but stayed where he was, quiet and motionless.

Another half-hour passed before the door opened again, and

The Hypocrite

this time Smythe had no doubt that the large body framed in the dim light from the interior was Browne. Smythe didn't know it, but Browne made a habit of taking a nightly stroll down to the cove and the warehouse where the merchant ships that navigated the Connecticut River unloaded before heading north to Hartford and Windsor.

Typically drunk during his nightly sojourn, Browne believed his walk helped him avoid the worst hangover maladies the next day. It was obvious from his lurching gait that tonight was no exception.

He passed a few dozen yards from Smythe's position, but his eyesight was nowhere near as good as his new partner's, and he was far too drunk to care. Nonetheless, Browne was determined to walk the half-mile or so to the cove, and then back before heading to his bedroom on the second floor of the tavern.

Smythe watched for another minute, then quietly arose and headed in the same direction. There was no one to see him, but if they had, they might have noticed that he picked up a large stone and carried it with him. It was as wide across as the palm of his large hand and smooth from years on the bottom of a crick bed, washed over by the endless flow of water.

Smythe couldn't make Browne out in the darkness any longer, but every so often he heard a scrape as Browne lurched into some object or another. Once or twice Smythe picked up on Browne's location from a muffled cough.

He passed the houses of the new captains of industry, the same ones he walked past earlier in the evening. But this time there were no voices, no lights and no cooking aromas. There was little to nothing to do at night here, and the inhabitants already were in bed.

The row of houses ended a few hundred yards from the cove, and after that the well-worn dirt street changed quickly to a rutted wagon track leading straight to the warehouse. The sides of the track were covered in dense brush that occasionally gave way to a steep bank on the cove side, and he could glimpse the water through the openings. The warehouse was built to accommodate horses and wagons on the land side, with the dock stretching well out into the cove on the water side.

Although the front entrance was at ground level, the land quickly sloped away heading toward the cove side of the building, dropping down a dozen feet or more. The Connecticut River was still tidal in this area and in the daytime it was easy to see the water marks left by the high tide.

At the moment, however, the tide was out, and the drop to the water line was littered with debris and rocks of all sizes and shapes. Smythe knew this from his brief reconnaissance of the warehouse and the dock earlier in the evening.

Smythe quickened his pace and came upon Browne so fast in the dark that he nearly bumped into him. Browne was relieving himself, and didn't see or hear Smythe.

He resumed walking the last fifty yards toward the warehouse, lurching unsteadily from side to side of the path. Smythe recalled that at one point the path was only a few feet from the edge of the cove, and that the drop in that location was especially high, with a scramble of rocks at the bottom.

As Browne neared this point, Smythe stealthily approached him from behind, and just as Browne lurched one last time toward the edge, Smythe hit him with the rock he carried, catching Browne in the temple with a powerful and sickening thud.

Browne made no noise as he pitched headlong over the edge and another thud was heard a second later as his body smashed into the rocks below. Smythe slipped behind some bushes along the path, watching and waiting to see if anyone heard Browne fall and would come to investigate.

The Hypocrite

After a few minutes, satisfied that he was still absolutely alone, Smythe crossed the path, and made his way down the bank. Browne's body lay still and crumpled, half in the water. Smythe checked to see if he was breathing or had a pulse, neither of which seemed to be the case.

Nonetheless, Smythe lifted Browne's head twice in his hands, and both times drove it with all the force he could muster, temple-first onto a large rock. Smythe could make out the stain of blood on the rock, and after the second time he thought he could see brain matter too, but he wasn't sure.

Smythe pulled Browne's body a few feet closer to the water, making sure his now dented head was lying on a rock. By morning his body would be submerged, and with any luck, the fish, crabs and other bottom feeders that moved in with the tide would start working on it.

Smythe again waited and watched, ensuring that no one saw him. Finally he slipped into the water, and began a short swim that took him behind and away from the row of houses that lined the street to the cove. He had crossed a small stream that fed the cove when he entered the settlement earlier in the evening, and he made for that, knowing it would allow him to leave the cove without dragging himself through the muck that settled in areas where the water flowed slowly or not at all.

When he reached the stream Smythe stayed in the current, taking the unusual action of completely washing his clothing. He didn't know when the body would be found, but if it was before he had a chance to give himself a complete going over in the daylight, he wanted to be sure that there was no evidence of Browne's brains or blood left on him.

When he was certain he was clean, Smythe continued upstream

The Hypocrite

to a point where the bank was firm. He exited, quietly made his way to his camp, and after one last check, wrapped himself in his blanket and quickly fell fast asleep.

Dawn breaks before 5 a.m. in that part of the world in summer, and it is preceded at least a half-hour earlier by the awakening of song birds. The first few chirps can quickly grow to a cacophonous din, and it was to this chorus that Smythe awakened some six hours later.

As the light grew he left his blanket and after patrolling the small perimeter of his camp, ensuring that he was quite alone, again gave his clothes a complete going over, stripping down until he was naked so he could inspect every inch of them. He noted with satisfaction that not only was there no evidence of his crime on his clothing, there was no blood or other bodily fluids on his hands or arms either.

Smythe had carried the rock he used to smash Browne's head with him as he swam across the cove. Halfway across he let go of it, certain that in the deep water it would never be found.

Satisfied that no other evidence existed, Smythe returned to his blanket, again falling fast asleep in a matter of minutes.

The sun was high in the sky, still well before noon, but certainly at least mid-morning when Smythe again awoke. He repeated his routine of earlier in the morning, again checking every square inch of his clothing and body, again concluding that nothing would connect him to Browne's death.

Gathering his belongings Smythe strode purposely toward the settlement. He broke out of the forest and made straight for the tavern, entering at a strong pace, his head up, his eyes gleaming, his demeanor assertive.

Smythe took in the tavern common room as he did the night before, noting with satisfaction that only the barmaid was there. It was too early for "dinner" the biggest meal in the colonial day, and a

The Hypocrite

bit late for breakfast, even for the merchants who already were showing themselves to be different from, and in their minds better than, the common colonialists.

"Well, good morning mistress," Smythe greeted the barmaid. "And where is my partner this good morning? I hope he hasn't forgotten that there is a new voice in the affairs of this establishment."

"I haven't seen him," the barmaid responded. "It isn't like him at all to be late. But none of the regulars have seen him and he doesn't answer my knock at his door."

"Well, perhaps he had business outside to attend to. I'll wait for him."

Smythe took a chair at the nearest table and for the first time took a close look at the barmaid. She was not exactly a beauty, but she wasn't unpleasant to look at either. She went about the task of preparing for the expected dinner customers, not appearing to take any special interest in Smythe, but giving him a closer examination when the opportunity presented itself.

She was slender, but not sickly, and effortlessly carried full buckets of water and moved barrels of ale into place behind the bar.

Suddenly hungry Smythe asked for and received a portion of that morning's breakfast, a warmed-over bowl of oatmeal mush and a tankard of ale. He realized he didn't know her name, an oversight that would have to be corrected immediately if she was going to work for him.

"What's your name mistress?" Smythe called across the room.

"Tess, master," she replied.

"Tess. That is a pretty name."

"Thank you m'lord," she responded. She waited a moment to see if Smythe intended any further conversation. With nothing more forthcoming she asked, "Will there be anything further m'lord?"

The Hypocrite

"Not at the moment," he replied. Tess went back to her work and paid no further attention to Smythe.

Smythe appeared intent on consuming his mush when a commotion was heard outside, first on the far side of the green, then moving closer to the tavern. Within a minute a small crowd burst inside, and by the way they took charge it was obvious they were the leaders of the community.

The leader of the group was tall, lean, and serious looking. He could have passed for Elder Clarke in Windsor and for a moment Smythe thought he had been tracked to Wethersfield.

The newcomer briefly glanced in Smythe's direction but then moved straight to where Tess was working.

"Mistress Tess, we have some news," he said with an uncommon gentleness. "Your patron Mr. Browne has just been found lying underwater in the cove."

Tess reacted as though she had been struck, and was led to a chair where she sat for a few minutes, composing herself.

"Is he dead?" she finally asked.

"Quite."

For the next hour the group questioned Tess about Browne's behavior the previous evening while relaying the story of finding him dead and the condition of his body. She told them that Browne was drinking heavily, and that his intake actually increased after he lost a half-interest in the tavern to Smythe.

They turned as one to Smythe, asking him pointed questions about his origins, which he replied to with answers that were vague at best, telling the lie that he recently arrived from New Haven, and planned to do business in the community. At that time in its history Wethersfield was a community of farmers and traders, and Smythe's story was not unlike that of many others who moved there.

The Hypocrite

It helped his credibility that Smythe had been to New Haven, just as he had been to Hartford and Windsor. He omitted telling the particulars of his arrival and departure from those communities, however.

Tess confirmed that Smythe left the tavern a good half-hour before she did, which also would have ensured he was long gone when Browne took his nightly stroll. Two of the village elders left to check out Smythe's story about sleeping the previous night in his campsite, returning a half-hour later to report that they visited the site and found nothing amiss.

In the end the group concluded that Browne's penchant for drinking and taking a nightly walk in the dark did him in, and that he staggered off the trail, falling to his death on the rocks at low tide.

The Puritan ethic was a major factor in this community as it was in Windsor, and several of the elders voice the opinion that "it is the will of the Lord Almighty." No one disputed that observation and finally the elders left, satisfied that they did a thorough job of investigating Browne's death.

The senior elder stopped for a moment before leaving, telling Smythe, "It appears that Master Browne's misfortune has worked out well for you. We have a thriving and sober community here. It would be well for you to remember that as you attend to business here."

"I wouldn't have it any other way," Smythe assured him, adding "the Good Lord works in mysterious ways."

"He certainly does," the elder observed dryly, then left without another word.

Smythe waited a decent interval, and then turned to Tess. "Tell me about yourself," he commanded.

"I am an indentured servant," she replied. "I arrived from England three years ago to work for Master Browne. I worked in a pub in

The Hypocrite

England and had the skills he needed to help him make this establishment turn a profit. I have four years left on my contract."

Smythe continued his questioning, determining that she was living in a small servants' room in the attic of one of the homes nearby, preferring that arrangement to living in the tavern with Browne. Browne was a bachelor, she told him, and had no living relatives that she knew of, nor did he leave a will.

Smythe walked upstairs, checked out the four rooms above the tavern, and then returned. He approached Tess, standing directly in front of her, much less than an arm's length away. He slowly reached out, lifting a strand of hair from her cheek.

"It would appear that I have inherited all of Master Browne's property, including you Tess. But you and I could make different accommodations," he suggested. Tess didn't answer, but didn't move away either.

"It would work out much better if you moved in here," he said. "Perhaps you and I could run this establishment together."

Again, Tess didn't respond, but again, she didn't pull away. Her mind was racing as she considered her options. Smythe appeared to have all the cards. He could make her stick to her contract with Browne, or he could fire her and order her off the property. If that happened Tess would quickly be in dire straits.

She had saved a little money since coming to work here, but not much, certainly not enough to support herself for an extended period. Her prospects for finding a husband in the community weren't all that bright either.

Tess made a point of living with another family, but it was generally assumed that Browne hired her for duties beyond those involved in cooking and serving drinks. In fact, he forced himself on Tess several times over the previous three years but she never re-

The Hypocrite

ported it to anyone, partly because of her fear of being cast out of the community, partly due to shame over his attacks, and partly because she was a strong woman in many ways and had her own method of dealing with his advances.

During the times he attacked her Tess forced her mind to focus on other, happier times, in far more pleasant places, succeeding to such a degree that she never moved while he was with her, and often was so far removed mentally from what was happening to her body that she didn't know when he finished and left.

Smythe wasn't much to look at but he was better than Browne. Tess considered all of this and one other factor while Smythe gazed at her, waiting for a response. If she took Smythe's offer and moved into the tavern, she felt certain she could successfully maneuver him to marry her.

Smythe was getting on in years, and she would have been lying if she said she did not consider that he just might have a difficult time keeping up with her.

If she married Smythe, and he was to die from over-exertion, she would inherit the tavern and all of its business. A widow, especially a well-to-do widow, was in a far better position to attract a husband than a single barmaid, and Tess knew it. She looked up at Smythe and smiled slightly.

"I said, I think you should recover your belongings and bring them here to the tavern." Smythe said. For the first time in his life he thought of a Smythe dynasty.

"As you wish, m'lord," Tess responded.

"That is it exactly, and that is exactly as it will be" Smythe said as she turned toward the door. "As I wish."

Chapter 1

Present Day—The American Dream

Bruce McAllister would never have walked through the door at Smythe Partners Ltd., or even answered the firm's ad for a creative writer if it hadn't been for September 11, 2001.

He watched the unfolding horror on television in his home office, believing at first that there would be death and some damage to the buildings, but the country would recover. Then, in what seemed like mere minutes, both towers of the World Trade Center collapsed in a maelstrom of dust, fire and debris.

McAllister was in his late twenties, single but dating. After a couple of years in the print media he was working as a freelance writer, providing marketing, advertising and media releases to his clients. Most of them were inextricably linked to those buildings. They either worked in them or served clients of their own who worked in or near the Twin Towers. Even if everyone he knew there had survived, their businesses would not.

In those early days McAllister didn't even think about the ultimate impact the attacks would have on him and others like him.

The Hypocrite

People died, were injured, horribly burned and lost loved ones. He was alive, far from Ground Zero that day. McAllister believed that he would recover from whatever minor affliction came his way, simply because he knew it to be true.

McAllister took a few days after 9/11 to finalize his assignments, then left for the Marine recruiting station in Hartford, Connecticut to enlist. He signed up for a delayed entry program that gave him a little longer to arrange his affairs, but took his physical and a battery of written exams that first day.

In early 2002 he raised his right hand, just before leaving for boot camp, swearing to uphold and defend the Constitution of the United States of America against all enemies foreign and domestic. Many years would pass before he returned home—years that included recruit training at Parris Island, South Carolina, then training as a machine gunner on armored personnel carriers.

McAllister felt that while his service wasn't preordained, it also wasn't a total shock. His father served in Vietnam and survived thirteen months of heavy combat. McAllister didn't intend to walk in his father's footsteps. But, he knew it would take a great combination of luck and skill to get through three tours in Iraq. Nonetheless he felt honor-bound to do something to help his country fight back ... and fight he did.

The battles in Afghanistan were over by the time he finished boot camp and his initial training, but then came the invasion of Iraq, and he was ready for it.

McAllister fought on the march to Baghdad, then in both battles in the city of Fallujah. By 2006, on his second enlistment, McAllister was again stationed in Iraq's Anbar province where the Marines were the one bright spot in a war that was unwinnable according to American politicians.

The Hypocrite

The Internet and cell phones enabled Marines to know that some in Congress compared their service unfavorably to Vietnam. The desk jockeys in the nation's capital were using rewritten Vietnam war history to conveniently ignore political elements in the mid-Seventies that betrayed the military—who never lost a single major engagement there—and the similarities were not lost on the Marines in Iraq.

McAllister meanwhile, was in the middle of the battle. During his tours he shot thousands of rounds at enemy positions from his .50-caliber machine gun, killed an unknown number of the enemy and saw several of his own friends die, too.

Between 2003 and 2007 as the war bogged down, McAllister came to distrust politicians. He and his fellow Marines knew they could defeat the Islamic terrorists if their hands were untied and they were allowed to do their jobs. He regularly exchanged emails with his Dad, often discussing the asinine rules of engagement that were costing the lives of American troops and resulting in the unwarranted arrests of many others. The terrorists laughed at them.

Along the way, McAllister also became distanced from his childhood religion—Christian Protestant. He didn't stop believing in God or Jesus. He stopped believing in organized religion and he stopped attending services. Every time a Marine or soldier was killed the chaplains would appear on the scene to offer words of comfort and exhortations to continue the battle against an enemy that fought by no rules.

As the casualties mounted, he wondered why the chaplains didn't turn their considerable verbal skills on Washington, and tell the American public what was happening due to political interference. "Who do they report to," McAllister asked himself, "God or Congress?"

The Hypocrite

In time, if he felt a need to converse with God, McAllister did it privately, in his own way, on his own time. He never became sacrilegious or anti-religious, he just withdrew from the formalities.

For all that he experienced in Iraq McAllister was never wounded, never outwardly affected by combat. He didn't think much about that, simply acknowledging that there are laws of physics—including force and trajectory—in addition to laws of probability and laws that are written by a higher authority. He tended to believe in the latter.

McAllister also never questioned his decision to join the Marines. "Not everyone can or should be in the military," his father taught him. "I'd rather a person is aware of that up front and does something else to contribute, than to go where they shouldn't be and endanger themselves and everyone around them."

McAllister was well-equipped to be in the military. He earned a few medals and was proud that he stood his ground, did his job well, and provided the heavy machinegun fire on target when it was needed. But he also observed American civilians working alongside the troops in Iraq, eating the same food, living in the same conditions, taking the same chances.

He had great respect for many of the civilian workers and tried not to dwell on the fact that they made far more money than he did. He concluded somewhere along the way that serving wasn't always defined by serving in the military, it was about doing something.

McAllister decided after two enlistments that his time in the Marines was over. He was discharged in early 2009 and returned to Connecticut. In the years since he left, McAllister married the woman he was dating when the War on Terror began, a lithe, shapely blonde named Julia, and during a period between deployments they purchased a home out in the country, east of Hartford.

With Julia working and his salary from the Marines they had

The Hypocrite

sufficient funds for the mortgage, taxes and routine expenses, as well some for savings, especially when he was overseas. But it didn't take him long after his discharge to see the dismal state of the country—people by the millions were unemployed and jobs were scarce.

Against this backdrop, McAllister began rebuilding the business he had established nearly a decade earlier while finding a paying job doing much the same work.

He began each day by scanning the help wanted ads in the state's newspapers, circling those that looked promising and then calling for an appointment. His resumé was solid in some respects, but many employers did not consider his time in the Marines as an asset. Often when he did get a solid lead, McAllister found himself in the company of dozens of other applicants for the same position.

The job search went on for several months, and ultimately, he came across an ad for a position with Smythe Partners, Ltd. It wasn't exactly what he planned to do, but at least it was in the general field. The job consisted of limited copy writing for a small packaging business in Rocky Hill, a mid-sized community across the river.

The position paid reasonably well, the commute wouldn't be horrible, and frankly, Julia was becoming increasingly uneasy as their savings dwindled away.

Still, if he had known what awaited him, McAllister would have avoided Smythe Partners, Ltd., like the Plague, because anyone who has the knowledge and ability avoids the Plague.

Chapter 2

Smythe Partners—The Interview

McAllister examined his reflection in the bathroom mirror, checking his shave, his haircut, his tie. His collars were starched and white, each button in place. The knot in his tie was perfect. His hair was trimmed only two days earlier and looked neat and natural, with just the slightest hint of new growth forming on the back of his neck.

He stood five feet, ten inches tall, still had the trim look of a Marine. His eyes were a steely blue and his hair was a variation on light brown, dark blond. He worked inside but still maintained the ruddy hue of a man who spends as much time outdoors as possible.

Everything seemed perfect on the outside, yet worrying that he may have missed something, he turned away from the bathroom vanity, walking into the master bedroom where a full-length mirror hung on the back of the entrance door. Standing before that mirror he again gave himself a thorough going over.

McAllister conducted myriad personnel inspections when he was an NCO in the Marines, one of many military experiences that stood him in good stead later. He scrutinized his suit jacket looking

The Hypocrite

for dangling threads—known as Irish Pennants in the Marines—and finding none, continued scanning down, checking the creases in his trousers and the 'break' at the bottom where the cuff met the top of his shoes.

The creases were knife-edge sharp, the breaks were just right, and in the back, the bottom of the cuff met the top of the heel on his shoes. There was not a speck of lint to be seen and finally, after one last, but very thorough examination, front and back, he was satisfied and turned away.

McAllister walked out the bedroom door, across the adjacent landing, then down the oak-plank staircase. On the first floor he traversed the great room, skirting the wood-burning fireplace and its ashes, giving wide berth to the sleeping family dog, a short-haired Lab mix, and entering the kitchen where a steaming cup of coffee, light, no sugar, was waiting for him.

His wife, Julia, looked up from a book she was reading at the kitchen table and gave him an appreciative once-over.

"You clean up nice," she teased. "Try not to spill any coffee on that shirt and tie. I worked hard to get those collars the way you like them."

McAllister made a face, teasing back, but nonetheless grabbed a paper towel from the rack over the countertop and carefully tucked it into his collar. He took a sip of the coffee, let it slide over the back of his tongue and let out a satisfied, "Ummm," as he swallowed.

"Coffee's good this morning," he said. "What did you do different?"

Julia made a gesture along the lines of tossing her cup at him, but laughed. The joke was old, nearly as old as their marriage, but it still played out several times a month, and it still worked.

"Are you ready?" she asked.

"I think so," he responded. "I haven't been on a real job interview

The Hypocrite

in quite a while. In fact, I haven't had more than a half-dozen my whole life, so this isn't exactly a routine for me."

"I know," Julia replied. "I packed your briefcase for you. Your resumé and letter of application are in the manila folder on top, and your writing samples are in the green folder."

"Did you include that list of references I drew up?"

"Sure did. I put that other list of your work history in there too, just in case you need it. Put in some naked photos of you too – just in case you're interviewed by a woman."

"Good job," he replied with a smile. He continued to sip the coffee and gazed out the kitchen window toward the back yard. Late March in eastern in Connecticut still clings to the cold, explaining why more than a dozen small birds flocked around the bird feeder, making quick work of the seed he had placed in it the night before.

McAllister went over his mental checklist three or four times, looking for any flaw, any inconsistency, any omission. He found none, so he finally relaxed, just a bit, satisfied that he was ready.

"Do you want another cup of coffee before you go? Or one to take with you?" Julia asked.

"No—thanks. They'll probably offer me one during the interview, and it would be just my luck to have someone smack into my rear bumper at a light just as I'm taking a sip."

Retracing his steps through the great room, he stopped at a coat rack by the front door, donning his overcoat and picking up his briefcase. He checked inside one last time, again going down the mental list, peering inside the flap underneath the cover to be sure a pen and note paper were included, and again finding all in order, snapped it shut. The leather briefcase measured two inches thick, with brass clasps and locks. He had owned it for more than a decade, but it wore well and he wouldn't have replaced it on a bet.

The Hypocrite

Bruce turned to Julia one last time, "Wish me luck, give me a kiss and I'm outta here."

Julia did as he asked, and walked him outside. "Call me on my cell when you're done. Don't wait until you get home. I want to hear how you did."

"I will," he promised, and walked across the front porch, heading for his truck in the driveway.

Julia didn't say it, but he knew she was worried about the cash flow. Everything seemed so good just a few months before, then the economy tanked, jobs became scarce and their financial world changed. Like many other Americans, McAllister was dealing with a widening recession while his income dwindled from a healthy flow to a mere trickle that didn't even cover the monthly bills.

Julia had always done her part, working for years as a bookkeeper at a small firm nearby. But even when they were both working it took their combined efforts to pay the bills and have enough to put away for retirement and emergencies. To make matters worse, her boss cut her hours to thirty per week a couple of months earlier.

Even while the economy was tanking, the country was still fighting the War on Terror. The long-term costs of war along with the bursting of the housing bubble started a financial chain reaction of collapse that still continued.

McAllister often thought of 9/11, nearly a decade ago now, and felt eternally grateful that he hadn't been in New York City and that none of his previous clients had been in the World Trade Center when it was hit. But virtually every one of them had ties to those buildings, and when the buildings collapsed, so did the work.

Two hitches in the Marines and his three tours in the war zone separated him from his previous life by many degrees. Getting back into the groove of civilian life was proving harder than he expected,

The Hypocrite

but he never complained about it. People died that day, thousands of people. Lives had been changed forever, in far worse ways than anything he was experiencing, and knowing that some survivors would never recover from the trauma bothered him deeply. But there were repercussions, and simply understanding how lucky he was didn't reduce the pressure of his responsibility to get back to work.

McAllister stepped into the cab of his pickup and placed the briefcase on the passenger seat. The truck was a well-kept older model Ford F-150. The interior was tidy, but also showed the wear and tear of use over the years. A forensic inspection of the floor rugs would have revealed sand from Rhode Island beaches, sawdust and bark from working in the woods, and even a few dog hairs from the times he transported his Lab to the vet.

Until very recently McAllister could have purchased a new truck if he wished. But he was a stickler for finding good vehicles, and keeping them long beyond the norm for American car buyers. He didn't see any point in getting rid of something he liked, in favor of something newer, just because it was newer.

He turned the key and the engine caught instantly, quickly settling into a smooth, nearly soundless purr. He pushed in the clutch shifting into reverse. The four-on-the-floor manual transmission was essential even though an automatic transmission made driving easier. After years of driving trucks in the woods, McAllister held the irreversible opinion that in lower New England a manual shift functioned far better in the winter than an automatic transmission ever could—and eliminated the need for four-wheel drive.

Icy sleet hits as frequently in this area as snow, and four-wheel drive is of no use on ice. Controlling the vehicle mattered greatly to him, and if he needed more traction when it snowed, he kept a ready supply of bagged sand and split wood to toss into the pickup bed for extra weight.

The Hypocrite

He backed out of his parking space, drove to the end of his driveway, turned left and accelerated smoothly through the gears. At a stop sign a half-mile away he turned left again and headed toward Hartford. Within twenty minutes McAllister was on Route 2, which would take him to Interstate 84, Interstate 91 and downtown Hartford if he wished. After a short ride he left the rolling countryside and pastures, a feature of eastern Connecticut, and entered spacious suburbs.

Ten minutes outside Hartford on Rt. 2, McAllister headed off the exit for Rt. 3, driving across the Connecticut River and I-91, ending up in Wethersfield. He drove as far as the Silas Deane Highway, a four-lane commercial route running between the south end of Hartford and Rocky Hill, south of Wethersfield. The Silas Deane teemed with businesses large and small, and traffic was usually heavy. The improved and widened section of Route 3 ended at a traffic light where McAllister turned left on the Silas Deane, driving about a mile before turning left again onto Parsonage Street, heading east.

In time, McAllister would learn the back streets and knock about ten minutes off his trip, but this day he was using directions from an Internet site, and he followed them exactly as they instructed. He quickly found himself at the intersection of Old Main Street in a relatively residential area.

Spotting the address, he pulled into the parking lot of a large, two-story brick building. The sign out front proudly proclaimed Smythe Partners, Ltd. McAllister had no way of knowing that Smythe Partners was only Moran Smythe, and he wouldn't have cared much if he did know. The parking lot was nearly full, but there were several empty slots. McAllister took casual note that a single space was set off well to the rear of the lot, and it was occupied by what appeared to be a late model Lexus.

He had total confidence he could convince his interviewer he was

The Hypocrite

the best man for the job. The personality of the interviewer and the culture of this advertising company were not on his mind at the moment. It only mattered that he bring in some money again, and quickly—thus his primary concern was the company's solvency. All else would take care of itself, or so he thought.

During his years in the Marines, Bruce McAllister saw many commanding officers and senior noncoms come and go. Career Marines sometimes expressed concerns about the command style of the newcomers, usually because they had grown accustomed to the rhythms of their previous commanders. But McAllister soon realized that as long as he did his job, and did it with the expertise expected of him, the changes in command had very little real impact on his life. There were exceptions of course, but as a rule, he did his job and they did theirs.

He also saw changes in management in his many civilian occupations. McAllister worked at numerous jobs while attending four years of college, some on summer vacations and others when his class loads were light. He became a writer almost by default.

McAllister found through trial and error that he had a gift for communication, spoken or written, and a wealth of life experiences that merged well with diverse audiences. After graduation he worked in the news business and saw changes in upper management. As corporate buyouts absorbed the old locally owned newspapers many of his colleagues experienced difficulties reacting to new management styles. Colleagues often remarked on his immunity to stress caused by management changes, and at other times they said ice water ran in his veins as deadlines approached.

McAllister met some of his old colleagues for lunch after his discharge and they brought up his cool demeanor under pressure. When asked how he remained so cool on deadline or when the corporate world was going berserk, McAllister responded with absolute serious-

The Hypocrite

ness, "No one was shooting at me."

Some took that remark as cavalier, and pointed out that he didn't have to worry about hostile fire in the years before joining the Marines.

"I'm not being arrogant," McAllister replied "I simply have different priorities." Some of his former journalism colleagues looked upon his decision to enter Marine training with disdain. Their attitude insured he would never return to the media. In truth, the Marines prepared him very well for the pressures of performance in corporate America.

The job at Smythe Partners, producing text for business packaging, was simple but still would require a decent level of creativity and ability to work on deadline. McAllister was good with a quip or pithy comeback. He figured his knowledge of the English language and ability to write one-column sized headlines for news briefs would help him here. Grabbing the briefcase from the passenger seat, McAllister stepped from the truck and took a last look at his tie and hair in the reflection from the driver's side window. He headed up the walkway toward the front door where a large stone step, probably taken from one of the many quarries in the area, and a brass doorknob and handle greeted him. A shiny brass plaque centered just above eye level said, "Smythe Partners, Ltd. Main Entrance."

He turned the doorknob, opened the door, and stepped inside, finding himself face to face with the receptionist's desk, occupied by an obese woman. He immediately decided she could best be described as 'unique,' that is, if he were being kind. Otherwise, 'weird' might have been a better description, but even that was just scratching the surface.

Stepping toward her desk, McAllister gave the room a once over. It was fairly wide and open, with cream-colored paint on the walls, an industrial drop ceiling overhead, and a closed door at the right rear. A glass door at the left rear of the room led into a meeting room, resem-

The Hypocrite

bling a greenhouse that gave him a view of the backyard. There, two large, barren maple trees held numerous, very busy bird feeders .

The usual contingent of file cabinets took up most of one wall. Scattered about were a few pictures and even some potted ferns. But the central feature of the room, after the receptionist's desk, was a large, black, wrought-iron spiral staircase that ascended to the second floor.

"May I help you?" The receptionist, whose nameplate at the front of an inordinately neat desk said Gail Lemming, smiled disingenuously. Her voice projected a raspy tonality, like a 1930's movie star vamp.

Lemming resembled an elongated version of a corner mail box, thick and square, yet tall with a wide nose, thick lips, at least two extra chins. Wisps of shocking red hair peeked out from under winter headgear that looked like a navy watch cap. She was wearing a long unbuttoned overcoat, a heavy gray sweater under that, along with a gray scarf hanging limp over her shoulders.

It was chilly outside, but comfortable inside and McAllister decided that she must suffer from an extreme sensitivity to the cold. Lemming stood to shake his hand and he noticed that she was wearing a gray skirt, and leggin's that were either overly thick, or were covering overly thick thighs and calves. A pair of black galoshes, with metal snaps, like the ones he wore to school in the winter when he was a child, rounded out her wardrobe.

"Hi. I'm Bruce McAllister," he said, removing his overcoat as he spoke. "I have an appointment to see Mr. Smythe about the writing job."

He hoped he didn't sound too anxious or too nonchalant. But before he could take the time to review his outward appearance, McAllister realized that Gail Lemming wasn't interested in anything he was saying. In fact, she appeared to have only one interest at the moment, and that, based on her unwavering stare, was his crotch!

The Hypocrite

"Is he here?" was all that McAllister could think to say.

Lemming reluctantly pulled her gaze from his private areas, responding with a tone of annoyance, "Of course he's here. He's up in his office. I'll let him know you're here. Take a seat if you like."

McAllister thanked her and headed for one of two chairs placed along the wall. A small end table between them held a few trade magazines. There was no place to hang his overcoat and Lemming didn't offer to take it. He turned quickly to sit down and found that as he walked away from the desk, Lemming was checking out his butt! He would have burst out laughing, but the blatant lust on her face was more than a little unsettling, especially since he really needed this job and was just a minute or so from being interviewed.

McAllister did his best to ignore Lemming, setting his briefcase on the second chair and feigning interest in a magazine on hydraulic tools. The silence in the room reached the point of discomfort until he heard footsteps in the room upstairs, and then the metallic sound of shoes on the wrought-iron staircase.

Moran Smythe slowly came into view, feet first. His tread down the stairs was slow and heavy, one step at a time, with his body gradually emerging, but, due to his height, which McAllister estimated to be about six feet six or so, his head did not appear for what seemed an eternity. When it did, McAllister again had to stifle an urge to laugh.

Moran Smythe also had what only could be considered a unique appearance—tall, ungainly, with a thick mane of jet black hair, eyebrows to match, and he was stooped. He stood as Smythe reached the bottom step and extended his hand.

"Mr. Smythe? I'm Bruce McAllister. I'm here for the interview on the writing job."

Smythe looked at him for a long three or four seconds, then extended his hand too, but asked, "How do you know I'm Moran

The Hypocrite

Smythe?"

McAllister was surprised by the question, but covered it quickly.

"Actually, I don't. But the receptionist said you were upstairs and would be coming down, so I put two and two together."

Smythe shook his hand with a firm grip and murmured something about two and two not always equaling four. He gestured toward the staircase and indicated that McAllister should go first.

"We'll talk in my office," Smythe said. "It's the first door on the right at the top."

McAllister ascended the staircase, and quickly arrived at the wide upper landing where three doors led from it. He went straight to the door on the right and entered a spacious, well-lit office. He stopped a few steps inside the door, noticing a woman seated at a conference table on his left.

"Please, have a seat," Smythe said, entering behind him. "Would you like some coffee?"

McAllister declined the coffee, and took a seat at the table, across from the light-haired, not quite blond, woman of average height. While not classically beautiful, she was nonetheless pleasant to look at. She glanced briefly at McAllister as he sat down, but quickly averted her eyes and didn't greet him.

"This is The Wife," Smythe said, by way of introduction. "She'll be your editor if I decide to hire you. She is an English major and worked in magazines before joining me here."

For the second time in as many minutes McAllister found himself at a loss. How was he supposed to address this woman, and what on earth was her name? He decided that those questions would work themselves out in due time, and again focused on the interview.

From his standpoint it went very well. He had ready answers for Smythe's questions, samples ready for his inspection, and easily en-

The Hypocrite

gaged in light banter. They spoke of the writing profession, the various aspects of the industry, and McAllister's life experiences.

Throughout the interview The Wife sat silently, nodding in assent when her husband made a point, but staying completely out of the conversation otherwise. McAllister couldn't help but wonder why she was there.

In what seemed like far less time, McAllister realized that an hour had passed, and Smythe was wrapping up the interview. McAllister had a good feeling about his performance and actually enjoyed the less formal conversations that were interspersed throughout the interview.

Smythe touched ever so briefly on his military background. McAllister decided long ago that he would not follow the lead of other veterans who downplayed or tried to hide their military experience to gain jobs or promotions. He understood their motives, but he would rather not work in a place where his time in the military was looked upon with disdain.

His resumé listed his military service including his combat time in Iraq.

"I really feel sorry for you guys," Smythe said. "You won all the battles and got the shaft from the politicians."

"Well, I agree about the politicians," McAllister said. "But I've never considered myself a victim. There are lots of people out there who can be considered victims. Going back to the Vietnam War you have millions of Southeast Asians who were slaughtered by the communists—they were victims, especially since the military won every major battle and then the politicians screwed it up big time.

" It looked like we were going to suffer the same fate in Iraq, but The Surge took care of that. I'm not sure about Afghanistan though. Things seem to have come full circle there. Nonetheless, there are lots of victims, but I don't consider myself to be one of them."

The Hypocrite

"Be that as it may," Smythe retorted, "I think the veterans are one of the few real groups in this country that deserve the title Victim."

McAllister wisely let the conversation die there. Smythe was cordial, affable even, throughout the interview, but his demeanor took a noticeably hard edge when he thought McAllister was disagreeing with him.

When Smythe realized that McAllister was finished with the subject, he turned to his right.

"Wife! Do you have any questions? Anything to add?"

"No," she replied meekly. "He seems like a good fit for our office."

"Thank you," Smythe said brusquely. Then, "I do have one more question for you, however. What exactly would you bring to this company that others who applied for this job can't?"

McAllister took a few seconds to absorb the question before answering. He figured that others who applied for a writing job probably had some kind of history, either in the media, public relations or communications, all of which could potentially place them on equal footing. But he doubted that they served in the military, particularly in combat.

But when he answered, McAllister played his ace. "My last post in the Marines was at the barracks in Washington, D.C.," he replied. "When my enlistment was coming to an end, there were several people in high positions who talked to me about staying in, going to officer school and doing another hitch as a lieutenant."

"Why didn't you take it?" Smythe asked.

"Three combat tours are more than enough," McAllister answered. "Besides, bullets and bombs make no distinction between officers and enlisted. But I did leave on very good terms and some of the people I met in Washington are in procurement. Meaning, I can give us a link to potential government contracts. I doubt the other appli-

The Hypocrite

cants can do that, and I think those connections could be very helpful in this economy."

Smythe nodded, and started gathering the papers that were spread before him, which McAllister took as a sign that the interview was over. Smythe stood, and McAllister closed his briefcase and followed Smythe's lead.

Smythe put out his hand to shake, with a little more enthusiasm than the shake when they met downstairs. Then, rather than heading to the door, he indicated a framed verse from the Bible on the wall behind him.

"We live by that creed here," Smythe said.

McAllister recognized the verse. "John, three-sixteen," he said.

"Very good," Smythe said. "I take it you are a Christian?"

"I was raised in the Methodist Church," McAllister replied.

"There aren't very many Methodists in Connecticut," Smythe noted.

McAllister didn't reply and Smythe began walking toward the door.

"I think this interview went very well," Smythe said. "I'll be checking your references, and as soon as I am done there, I'll call and we'll talk money."

McAllister thanked him and walked outside to the hallway. Smythe made no effort to accompany him so he continued on down the spiral staircase.

At the bottom Lemming appeared to be finishing a phone call. She put the phone back in its cradle and turned toward McAllister, again giving him one of those direct stares that were quickly becoming unsettling.

"How did it go?" she asked, considerably more polite this time than she had been earlier.

The Hypocrite

"It seemed to go very well," McAllister replied. He didn't want to appear rude, but at the same time, if he was going to work here, he didn't want to create an atmosphere where Lemming automatically thought he would confide in her.

"You're the third person he interviewed," she said, with a barely suppressed giggle. Then, with a direct stare at his crotch, she added, "I hope they pick you!"

McAllister ignored the stare as best he could. "Well, thank you," he said. "I hope they pick me, too."

He said goodbye and opened the door to the outside. As he reached back for the handle to close the door he again noticed that Lemming was ogling his rear end, her eyes fixed, and her mouth agape.

McAllister gently closed the door, ignored her stare, and walked back to his truck. He got in, put the briefcase back on the seat, started the engine and put it in reverse. Out on the street he retraced the route he had taken coming in, and when he was in fourth gear, he put on the cell phone headset and called Julia.

"How did it go?" she asked before even saying hello.

"Ah, the wonders of Caller ID," he replied. "It seemed to go pretty well. The owner said he is going to call my references and then get back to me about money. I can't imagine anyone will be saying anything bad about me."

"That's great! Should I defrost a steak for dinner?"

"Not yet. We still have to discuss money and see if he makes a reasonable offer."

There was a noticeable letdown in Julia's voice as she agreed to wait, and McAllister was again reminded how on edge she was about this job.

"Hey, maybe by tomorrow," he promised. Julia reluctantly agreed.

"I'll see you in a bit and we can talk more," McAllister told her.

The Hypocrite

"At least we're over a big hurdle. And, I've got some things to tell you about this place that will crack you up."

He hung up then and concentrated on his driving. He was pulling into his driveway within a half hour, and after parking the truck, walked toward the house, loosening his tie as he went.

Julia met him at the entrance. "So, what other good things happened?"

"Give me a minute," McAllister protested. He shed his overcoat, then his jacket, placed his briefcase on the floor at the entrance to his office, just off the great room, and proceeded to the kitchen where the coffee pot was still plugged in and an "oldies" station was playing on the radio.

He poured a cup, added some half-n-half and sat at the table.

He gave Julia an overview of the office, and the types of questions Smythe asked during the interview. He also told her of the strangeness of The Wife, and her non-participation in the interview.

"I really don't know why she was even there," he said. "But this is the part that is going to crack you up. Literally from the minute I walked into the receptionist area downstairs, until I went upstairs for the interview, and for the half-minute or so it took me to walk out afterward, this receptionist kept staring at me."

"Staring how?" Julia asked.

"When she wasn't staring at my crotch, she was staring at my butt," McAllister told her.

"Does she have any influence in the hiring?"

"I don't think so. She wasn't in on the interview and Smythe never included her in anything. But that was just the weirdest situation. Between her and The Wife, it was just really odd." McAllister realized he was thinking out loud as much as having a conversation, but the events involving Lemming puzzled him and he needed to talk about it.

The Hypocrite

"So, you didn't have to use the naked pictures I put in the briefcase?" Julia teased.

"Yeah, naked pictures. I have the feeling they would have really gone over big—so to speak. Man, if I brought them out I probably would have been tackled!"

"Was she pretty?" Julia asked with what could only be described as a hit of slyness.

"No. Not pretty. Definitely not pretty. Un-pretty. Beyond un-pretty. You have nothing to worry about. But," McAllister teased her right back, "you better keep that body in shape, or you never know, I might be tempted."

Julia tossed a dish towel at him, and he ducked it laughing. McAllister finished his coffee and stood.

"I'm going to change and work out downstairs," he said. Julia nodded, said she was going to the store and asked if there was anything special he wanted for dinner.

McAllister deferred to her judgment on that and started through the great room.

He took one step but stopped and turned back toward her.

"Oh, one other thing. Smythe had a Bible verse up on the wall and made a special effort to point it out to me. I guess he's really religious or something. But he seemed impressed that I knew it."

"What was it?" Julia asked.

"John three-sixteen."

"And you knew it?" she asked. Julia knew that her husband attended church throughout his childhood, and he told her how most weeks he went to Sunday school before the regular service. He also took extensive religious training as a teenager before being confirmed as a member of the Methodist Church, and attended religious youth retreats, some for as long as a week, before he graduated from high school.

The Hypocrite

But from his first Iraq tour onward he stopped attending church regularly, and they didn't belong to a church in the community. They talked about organized religion on a surface level, and were pretty much on the same page concerning their feelings about it. Still, he surprised her sometimes with his memory of things he learned long ago.

"Yeah, I recognized it."

"From back when you were a kid?" she asked incredulously.

McAllister started chuckling, then burst into a full laugh.

"What's so funny about that?" Julia asked, with just a bit of annoyance beginning to show.

"I just realized that Smythe probably thought the same thing. That I know it from my upbringing."

"What's so funny about that?" Julia repeated, this time with far more than a hint of annoyance.

"Football," he said, still laughing nearly uncontrollably.

"Football? What is so funny about football, and what does it have to do with your job interview?" Now she was really annoyed.

"I didn't learn it from religious instruction when I was a kid. I learned it watching Sunday afternoon football, because someone was always waving a sign up in the stands that said John 3:16. So one day I looked it up. That's why I remembered it and that's why I said football."

By now Julia was totally disgusted, but against her own best efforts began laughing, too.

"That is too much. You can't ever tell him that, Bruce. Promise me you won't."

"I won't. I promise. I have a feeling it could get me fired. To tell the truth, I know we need the income, and I hope the money offer is good, but as I look back on it, the whole office situation has me a bit concerned."

The Hypocrite

Julia turned then and headed for the door, shaking her head in mock amazement, but still laughing.

"Go do your workout. I'm going to the store. I guess now I'll have to live with football as a job skill."

She closed the door and McAllister headed upstairs to change into his sweats. He had a small gym in the basement and as soon as he was changed he headed downstairs. He turned on the light and stepped onto his treadmill for a warm-up jog. In a minute McAllister's focus was on his heart rate and gradually his sense of unease diminished.

Occasionally, he would break into a wide smile and laugh again, but still, the nagging feeling kept creeping back. McAllister was confident he would get the job if the money offer was fair, but he learned in the Marines to look for the little things that can warn of impending ambush.

The interview was promising, but there were more than a few little things. He knew all too well that sometimes little things can add up.

Chapter 3

Something Amiss

It is weird how things turn out when you try your best, and your best is very good, but not quite good enough for someone with ulterior motives.

Bruce McAllister quickly proved his worth at Symthe Parnters Ltd., yet even four months after his hiring, he could never please Moran Smythe. No matter how much copy he turned out, no matter how quickly, no matter how well it pleased the clients, Smythe always had something negative to say.

McAllister hadn't waited long for the job offer. In fact, Smythe called him early in the evening on the same day he interviewed asking what McAllister wanted for a salary. Smythe came back with an offer that was nearly $20,000 lower. In normal circumstances, McAllister would have held out for a figure somewhere in the middle of what he wanted and the amount Smythe offered. But McAllister knew he had high-ended his first figure, and in the end, Smythe came up a little and McAllister came down a lot.

But he got the job and began working in mid-April. Paying the

The Hypocrite

bills regularly helped the McAllister household return to normal, and now, in mid-July, Julia was far more at ease. Their fears of being forced to sell the house subsided.

Work at Smythe Partners, Ltd. was fast paced and there was plenty of it. McAllister had no trouble fitting in and was turning out copy within a day of getting settled in his new office. In a sense his job was simple. His task involved creating words for the outside of packages designed by the graphics department that would entice the public to buy the product.

But there was an ocean of competition on the American market and the hard part was finding a way to make Smythe's clients stand out from the rest. McAllister was given a simple directive the day he started—create "sparkling" copy to enhance the visual packaging that surrounded clients' products.

The firm included sales, marketing and graphics departments in addition to a bookkeeper and the receptionist. There were a dozen employees in total, and most them worked in a block of offices to the rear of Lemming's desk on the first floor. Her immediate terrain was limited to the ten-by-twelve foot office at the front of the building. A door in the wall behind her led to a hallway that in turn led to four doors that opened into their respective departments. Aside from the entrance door, the only other outlet was the door at the far left that opened into the glassed-in conference room.

McAllister soon developed an affinity for eating his lunch in that room with its view of the well-landscaped yard and the bird feeders. The room created a sunny nook where many of the other employees also gathered at lunch time.

Most of the other workers were men, except for the bookkeeper and two of the graphic artists. The other men appeared to be a bit standoffish at first, a factor that McAllister finally realized stemmed

The Hypocrite

from professional jealously over his having an office versus the cubicles where they worked. That, however, soon turned out to be not such a beneficial arrangement.

McAllister's office was on the second floor, on the left side of the staircase, directly across from Smythe's office. One of the first things McAllister learned about his office, aside from its being the only other individual office in the building, was that Smythe's desk and chair were situated where he could look out his door and right at McAllister's desk. In fact, the way the furniture was arranged, Smythe could, and often did, look straight out of his office to the back of McAllister's head, and simultaneously at McAllister's computer screen.

It was easy at first to understand Smythe's presumed motives. After all, McAllister was a new hire, and despite his record and the enthusiasm of former employers and colleagues who gave him references, Smythe had no idea how McAllister would work out in the new position until he actually worked in it. Their employment agreement included a three-month probation period, and McAllister quickly decided that once the probation passed by a sufficient amount of time he would rearrange the office furniture, especially the desk.

This plan was reinforced on several occasions when McAllister found Smythe literally sneaking up on him to view his progress on the project of the moment. From McAllister's point of view, Smythe only had to ask what he was doing and McAllister would be happy to outline not only the work he was engaged in, but what he planned for the rest of the day too.

Eventually, McAllister passed his probation and within a couple of weeks rearranged his office. His back still faced Smythe's office, but there no longer was a direct view from one desk to the other, hence the game playing.

Smythe's habit of spying on him quickly evolved into a game of

The Hypocrite

cat and mouse, with Smythe attempting to enter the office and stand behind McAllister without his knowing about it, and McAllister picking up on Smythe's presence before Smythe could complete his mission.

But it didn't take McAllister long to realize that it wasn't a game. More than once Smythe made remarks about McAllister's being "a big tough Marine," and it wasn't said as a compliment.

It always came in the form of, "A big tough Marine like you should be able to hear a mere civilian like me before I get here."

McAllister assumed correctly that Smythe's derision had something to do with his avoiding the military and McAllister's service in the Marines. Smythe once remarked over lunch that he was mystified by the entire War on Terror run-down-to-the-recruiting-office-and-join-up response to the attacks on the country.

McAllister shrugged off the comments. "Probably just as well, Moran," he said. "There are enough of us dragging that anchor behind us as it is." But that didn't stop Smythe from commenting on what he believed was the proper audio abilities for the average Marine.

McAllister did hear Smythe every single time. But it was not because of his Marine service. Smythe was a good six inches taller than McAllister, and outweighed him by at least fifty pounds. Also, the combination of diesel engines, machine gun fire, and artillery that McAllister was exposed to in the Marines hadn't done his hearing any favors.

But for his entire life, McAllister, for reasons that he never understood, counted things. For instance, he knew the first day that there were fourteen steps on the spiral staircase coming up to the second floor. He knew that the eighth step was a tad loose and made a slight metallic rasp when it was stepped on.

He also knew that it was exactly sixteen normal steps from his

The Hypocrite

chair to the front of Smythe's desk, and that on the return trip, at step ten, a loose floorboard made a small but noticeable squeak. It wasn't the type of squeak that drew attention if you weren't paying attention or had gotten used to it, but it was there and McAllister knew it.

Since the wide colonial era variety board that caused the squeak ran perpendicular to the path of travel between the two offices, it didn't matter where it was stepped on to get it to squeak, thus it didn't matter if Smythe took long or short steps. When McAllister heard the squeak, he knew Smythe was coming, and he had a good idea of just how many seconds to wait before spinning around in his chair to confront the intruder.

Smythe never figured it out. McAllister quickly realized that Smythe was probably the most self-absorbed individual he had ever met, and that worked against Smythe when he was intent on such important matters as sneaking up on an employee.

McAllister often referred to the office as The Zoo. Occasionally at home, he would ponder the weirdness of it all, and why on earth a business owner, who had so much else to deal with, would make a big deal out of such a picayune matter. There was no figuring it out, he concluded, but it was decidedly weird.

Then in July, the routine took an even stranger turn.

McAllister was working on a project, and glanced over at the digital clock on his desk to gauge whether to move on to a new segment before lunch when he heard the familiar squeak. He counted to six, and then quickly spun around in his swivel chair to confront Gail Lemming!

Her presence just outside the office door surprised McAllister as much as discovering that she was behind him rather than Smythe. McAllister had not heard any movement in Smythe's office in some time. It suddenly occurred to him that Smythe had left the office some

The Hypocrite

twenty minutes earlier going down the spiral staircase without saying a word. It further occurred to McAllister that he never heard Smythe return. Meaning, Lemming was in Smythe's office when he left and quietly stayed there for the next twenty minutes.

One of McAllister's earliest lessons in Smythe Partners office politics came from the guys in the marketing department, who professed a universal loathing for Lemming. They invited McAllister to join them for a lunchtime pizza on a payday three weeks after he started at Smythe Partners. During the meal they revealed that they were all ogled by Lemming when first interviewed.

McAllister always shrugged off Lemming's unwelcome advances as a personality quirk, or more accurately, a personality defect, and took to avoiding her as much as possible. Since her considerable weight made it difficult for her to use the spiral staircase, she didn't often drag herself up to the second floor.

McAllister usually arrived at work before Lemming's starting time so avoiding her was not a daily issue. He passed her desk on the way out to lunch and again when he returned, but she was usually on the phone or otherwise engaged, so her direct stares and pointed suggestions were a rarity rather than the norm.

But Ken Wilson, the director of the marketing department, revealed that Lemming was far more than an occasional annoying ogler. She made direct advances to virtually every man in the office, he revealed that day at lunch, and when she was turned down, strange things occurred.

She rummaged through desks after everyone left for the night. Phone messages disappeared, and computer files mysteriously lost recent additions, or were relocated to obscure folders, and on occasion even deleted. The computer manipulations were possible because Smythe arranged the office network in such a way that one central

The Hypocrite

computer could control all the other work stations.

Anyone with the password to the central computer, who had the time and opportunity, could enter other computers further down the line. The pecking order started with Smythe, then progressed oddly enough through Lemming's computer which was set up second in line, and then on to the others.

The one difference in the network after Lemming's computer was from that point on it was configured as a parallel circuit, meaning she or Smythe could control all the other computers at will, but the employees in the other departments had control only over their own work stations. That meant if something weird happened on one work station in any department, it either was the result of someone toying with that machine directly, or Smythe or Lemming had tampered with the work.

Smythe repeatedly assured the employees that he and only he had the access code, but they all suspected that somehow Lemming gained access to it and used it to disrupt their work and accounts whenever she developed a grudge against them.

Wilson told McAllister that they noticed that every attack on their computers came at a time when Smythe was away from the office or in the evening. Male staffers, and only the male staffers, complained bitterly that on the morning after rebuffing advances from Lemming, they would come to work to find files in disarray or missing entirely.

Smythe twice called Lemming into his office and questioned her in front of the complaining staff member, but each time she disavowed any knowledge of their accusations and, lacking proof, she was off the hook. In both cases the staff members were let go soon thereafter and further complaints ended. But that didn't end the bitterness toward Lemming nor the certainty that she was the one who was tampering with their work.

The Hypocrite

McAllister made a mental promise to himself not to become involved in any confrontations with her. He also made backups every night before leaving the office of all files he was working on, and if a project was finished or in final draft form he forwarded a copy to Smythe for his review in the morning.

Thus far, his distance from Lemming prevented any unpleasantness between them and he didn't experience any problems with his files.

But now he was facing Lemming, who appeared both startled and quizzical, partly because he had spun around so fast, he guessed, but there was something more too.

"Can I help you Gail?"

"Moran wanted me to ask you if you were interested in staying in for lunch today?" she replied.

"But isn't he having lunch with the elders today?"

The "elders" were a half-dozen Christian evangelists who represented a growing church of believers that counted nearly 200 members. Smythe belonged to their church, was considered a member of the inner circle, and hosted a regular prayer luncheon in the sunroom.

Although other staffers were encouraged to use the room for meetings, conferences or their own lunches, it was off limits on the days the elders came to lunch, unless someone wanted to join the group. The lunch agenda was informal with time for prayer and Bible study as well as socialization.

McAllister met the elders within a few weeks of starting work, and liked them all. They were a sincere and earnest group he decided, and his own interest in the Bible, more from a historic than religious perspective, made them a ready source of productive conversation.

He knew they would like him to join in their meetings, and probably their church, but that was not in the cards for McAllister.

The Hypocrite

He had no qualms about discussing religion in general, the Bible in particular, and debating the fine points as well as the larger issues.

But far too often in his life, primarily in his own home when he was younger, and in his extended family more recently, McAllister saw religious discussions turn heated. Disagreements developed when people couldn't possibly know whether the point they were making was true or not. That's when the issue became the argument and the argument became the issue.

He decided long ago to keep his innermost feelings on religion to himself, and while he was very strong in his beliefs, he also avoided organized gatherings.

"Moran was hoping you'd join them," Lemming said, with what appeared to be an emphasis indicating it was more of a command than a request.

"Well, I appreciate the invitation, but I have some other matters to attend to during lunch," McAllister replied.

For a moment Lemming just stared at him, with unblinking eyes that reminded him of garter snakes stalking frogs in his yard. There was no emotion, and he wasn't sure there was understanding either. In fact it appeared that she couldn't compute how someone would turn down a command invitation.

"I'll let Moran know," she finally replied, with a sigh-like heave of her chest.

"I'll take care of it," McAllister said. "I'm sure he'll understand."

Lemming didn't reply, and instead turned toward the stairway, descending slowly and heavily, as if the weight of the world were on her shoulders.

McAllister watched her take one slow painful step at a time and then turned back to his work. But he found himself staring at his computer screen without really working. That he would be invited to a

The Hypocrite

prayer lunch really wasn't unusual, but the way the invitation was delivered seemed odd, and Lemming's reaction to his refusal was odder still.

McAllister had friends who were evangelists and they often invited him to their breakfasts or lunches. Sometimes he accepted and sat respectfully while each meal was preceded by a prayer, then enjoyed the ensuing conversation.

Efforts to convince him to join their organizations were an accepted part of the outing, but each time he declined and skillfully deflected the sometimes insistent requests. Ultimately he respected their views, but did not share their enthusiasm for more formal associations—formal as in a specific time, on a specific day each week, in a specific place.

McAllister finally gave up on doing any further work before lunch. He searched the downstairs for Smythe to let him know he wouldn't be making the lunch meeting, to no avail. Smythe was not in the front office, the glassed-in meeting room, nor in the back area where the marketing, sales, graphics and accounting people worked.

He figured Smythe stepped out to purchase drinks or snacks for the lunch. McAllister really did have an appointment that day with a banker nearby, who had agreed to consolidate the credit card bills McAllister amassed back when he wasn't working.

It wasn't a huge debt, but the fees and wholly unsatisfactory interest rates and payment plans that the credit card companies required would keep him paying off the debt for years longer than he would need to if he borrowed the same amount from a bank. As soon as he passed his probation period he applied for a consolidation loan at several area banks and today he was signing the papers.

As he exited Smythe Partners, McAllister met one of the elders from Smythe's church on the sidewalk. Derrick Simpson was a tall,

The Hypocrite

straight-backed, wiry man, with a shock of graying hair on his head that gave him the appearance of a church deacon.

He had a wry sense of humor that often verged on self-depreciation and a near-perpetual twinkle in his eye, although he could be stern on occasion, especially in matters involving morals. McAllister talked with him often, both on the days when he came to the prayer lunch at Smythe Partners, and on other occasions when Simpson dropped in to talk with Smythe about church business.

McAllister liked Simpson immensely and Simpson in return gave McAllister sufficient respect for his religious views by often inviting McAllister to join the group at lunch or to Sunday services at their church, but not pressuring him when McAllister invariably demurred.

"I hear you're finally going to join us for lunch today," Simpson said with a wide smile on his face.

McAllister was walking toward Simpson, but was noticeably taken aback by his statement—and it was a statement, not a question.

"Actually, no I can't," McAllister said. "I didn't even get the invite until ten minutes ago and I already have an important meeting with the bank. I just can't do it today."

"Well, that is certainly odd," Simpson replied after a short pause. "I spoke with Moran yesterday afternoon and he said you would definitely be there with us."

Neither man spoke for several seconds. Then Simpson seemed to recover, asking "Is everything all right with you? I mean, at the bank? You're not having any difficulties are you?"

"No, not at all," McAllister replied. "In fact it's just the opposite. I had some credit card bills from when I was unemployed, and I consolidated them once I went past my probationary period. I went to a few banks in the area and got the best deal they offered. I'm on my way over to sign the papers now. That's why I can't come to lunch."

The Hypocrite

"Terrific," Simpson responded. "It looks like the Good Lord is watching out for you!"

"I've never doubted that for even an instant," McAllister said. "I have to get going or I'll be late for my appointment."

He moved on and Simpson watched him for a moment before turning and walking inside Smythe Partners. He wore a frown in place of his usual pleasant demeanor and shook his head slightly just as he reached for the doorknob.

McAllister meanwhile headed back to the Silas Deane highway and within five minutes pulled into the parking lot at the bank. He exited his truck, walked in and moved to an area reserved for Customer Service. In less than a minute the bank manager, a slight, bespectacled, balding man with a pleasant but not exactly personable smile emerged from his office.

"Mr. McAllister," he said, more as a statement than a question. "Nice to see you again. Come with me please and we'll get started on your paperwork."

McAllister followed the manager into a glassed-in office that provided virtually no privacy. McAllister took a seat in a functional if unremarkable chair in front of a large mahogany desk that had plenty of room but surprisingly little in the way of clutter.

The manager pulled a file from a cabinet that matched and stood off to one side of his desk, and from the file pulled a sheaf of papers. The nameplate on the desk identified him as Erle Smith. "Everything appears to be in order," he intoned. "Did you bring your last three pay stubs?"

"Yes, I did," McAllister replied, taking them from his own folder, one that Julia had prepared for him the previous night and made sure he took with him that morning.

"And the letter from your employer confirming that you are still

The Hypocrite

working there?" Smith said with a quizzical look.

"What letter?" McAllister queried, feeling a bit of a jump in his pulse. "No one mentioned anything about a letter, just the three most recent pay stubs." He could feel the heat rising in his face as he spoke, and the flush of anger was accompanied by a knot in his stomach that something was going wrong here. He didn't want to return home that night with the news that the loan had not been approved.

"Oh, I am so terribly sorry," Smith said, with a tight, humorless grin. "The board of directors made that change at their meeting last month. Everyone who had a loan pending was supposed to be notified. I do apologize. Someone apparently dropped the ball on your account."

"Well, what can I do to resolve this?" McAllister asked. "I still want to finalize the loan today and I am still working there. That shouldn't be a problem to prove."

"Is there anyone at the office now?" Smith asked. "As long as I can get verbal verification for now you can return later or even tomorrow with the letter and I'll just add it to the file. I do apologize for the inconvenience."

"The office is open, the receptionist is on duty, and fortunately Moran Smythe is having lunch with a group of associates as we speak," McAllister answered. "I'm certain we can resolve this in just a few seconds," he added, handing his business card to Smith and pointing out the main number to the office.

Smith dialed the number, waited as it rang and the told the person who answered the phone on the other end, presumably Gail Lemming, "This is Erle Smith, manager of the First Institute of Savings here in Rocky Hill. I am calling to confirm the employment of Mr. Bruce McAllister with your firm. Can you give me your name and verify that he works there?"

The Hypocrite

There was a pause and then Smith repeated, "Bruce McAllister. I have pay stubs showing that he was working in your firm as of last week and I just want to confirm that he is still employed with you. That's right McAllister. M C A L L I S T E R." He spelled the name carefully and succinctly.

McAllister meanwhile was becoming more than a little agitated and worked to keep his feelings and his mouth in check. Finally he told Smith, "Put your phone on speaker, please. Let me speak to her."

Smith wordlessly pushed the speaker button and McAllister heard Lemming's voice saying, "Let me check our employment records. Can you wait just a minute?'

"Gail, it's me. Bruce," McAllister said with growing agitation. "Can you please confirm for Mr. Smith that I am still working at Smythe Partners? This is very important."

"Oh, Bruce! Nice to hear from you. I don't think I'm allowed to give out public information on current or past employees."

McAllister nearly burst a vein on that one, but kept his temper from exploding. From between very tightly clenched teeth he managed to tell Lemming "Look. I was at my desk fifteen minutes ago, and spoke to you then. I am coming back to work as soon as I am finished here. You know that, and I am giving you permission to tell that to Mr. Smith."

"Unfortunately, you aren't my boss and only Moran Smythe can decide whether that is permissible," Lemming answered, with cloying sweetness.

"Then get Moran to the phone please, and let him do it," McAllister responded curtly.

"Mr. Smythe is at a special luncheon with some colleagues and left word that he is not to be disturbed," Lemming said, again with all the sweetness of a pickpocket.

The Hypocrite

"I'll take the blame if he is upset!" McAllister spoke tersely, all but beside himself with anger over Lemming's conduct. He did everything in his power to maintain control over his emotions, especially since Smith now had a concerned look on his face that did not speak well for McAllister's loan application.

Back at the office, Lemming wordlessly put the phone on hold and waddled to the luncheon meeting. "Mr. Smythe," she said, interrupting the ongoing discussion, "Bruce McAllister is on the phone and he seems very upset about something. He needs to have his employment verified and I told him I'd be happy to do it. But he said it has to come from you, even after I told him you're not to be disturbed. He insists on talking with you."

Smythe stood with obvious irritation and stalked into the reception area. "Where is McAllister?" he demanded of Lemming.

"At some bank with a man named Smith," she answered with an innocent look and sweetness of tone.

Smythe snapped up the phone and punched the hold button. "This is Moran Smythe. With whom am I speaking?"

"Moran, it's Bruce McAllister. I'm at the First Institute of Savings finalizing some financial matters and I just need you to confirm that I am employed at Smythe Partners."

"Of course you're employed here. Why couldn't you just let Lemming tell that to the bank without disturbing me?"

"Well, I tried to, but she told the bank manager that only you could divulge that information."

At that point Smith interrupted. "Mr. Smythe. It's Erle Smith at the First Institute. I'm very sorry to have created a problem for you, but with your confirmation I have all the information I need. Thank you so much for your time."

Both McAllister and Smith were noticeably startled when

The Hypocrite

Smythe dropped the phone back into its cradle without saying goodbye. After the sudden and quite loud CLICK, Smith stared at McAllister for a long half-minute, or more to the point, stared through him.

Finally, he picked up a pen and began making little X's on the lines where McAllister was to sign. "That was highly unusual Mr. McAllister. I trust you'll be able to drop off the required letter tomorrow?"

"I'll stop by again at lunch time," McAllister answered. His blood pressure was subsiding and all he wanted now was the loan approved, signed off and the money deposited in his checking account at a bank across the river in Glastonbury so he could pay off his credit cards.

The next few minutes passed in a blur of forms, the only conversation being the occasional instruction from Smith, "Sign here, and here, and here," repeated as often as necessary until the stack of forms was completed.

Smith left the office, walked behind the teller counter, and returned a few minutes later with a check and a handshake. "Thank you, Mr. McAllister. It has been a pleasure doing business with you. If you like, I can open a new checking account for you with our bank. It will only take a few minutes and we can deposit your loan check directly into it."

McAllister thanked him, but declined the offer. Smith placed the check in a business envelope which itself was placed in a manila file folder and that in a larger envelope. McAllister took the package, shook Smith's hand again, and left the bank, with a feeling that was close to trepidation in his gut.

Smith watched him go, and finally shook his head in wonderment as he sat back down at his desk and picked up the folder for the next client in line.

The Hypocrite

McAllister fought a sudden urge to drive across the river and deposit the check in a branch of his bank. Instead he drove back to Smythe Partners, parked and headed into the office just as the elders were leaving.

Usually they were friendly and any chance encounters resulted in a good-natured bantering. But now McAllister was confronted only with curt nods and occasional frowns.

Even Simpson seemed to have lost his normal friendliness and barely spoke as they passed on the sidewalk. McAllister entered the building and was confronted by both Lemming and Smythe.

"Come with me," Smythe commanded. He headed toward the staircase with Lemming right behind him, meaning McAllister had to follow her all the way up—not exactly what he would have called a pleasant position.

Smythe was already seated in his office and, without waiting for McAllister to sit down, immediately demanded, "What was that all about? Why was I interrupted and why were you NOT at my lunch?"

McAllister told Smythe about the bank and Lemming's refusal to handle the verification herself, but Smythe cut him off in mid-sentence. "I don't need any inter-office politics here. If you two have problems work them out yourselves. And that doesn't explain why you missed a business lunch. I'm not especially pleased that you won't at least break bread with the elders of my church in a social setting, but you were told that this was business, not religion and you still wouldn't join us! Gail told me yesterday you'd be joining us and yet when I came back today expecting to see you at the table, you were nowhere to be found. Do you know how terrible that made this business look in the eyes of my friends, colleagues and potential customers? DO YOU?"

McAllister quickly responded that Lemming told him of the

The Hypocrite

luncheon only a few minutes before noon that day and he was NOT told that it involved business. But Smythe was hearing none of it.

"I find that very difficult to believe," he said, to McAllister's amazement. "Now get back in your office and try to do something productive and useful with the rest of the day."

McAllister turned without a word and went back to his desk, happy that he had rearranged the office layout and wouldn't have to feel Smythe staring holes through his back for the rest of the afternoon. He immersed himself in his work and was only barely aware of Smythe leaving the office about fifteen minutes before normal quitting time.

At 5 p.m. McAllister gathered his belongings, cleaned up his desk, closed his files, copied them to a flash drive, and headed downstairs. In the reception area Lemming was staring at him coldly. No one else was around.

"What was that all about today?" McAllister demanded.

"I have no idea what you're talking about," Lemming responded in a tone that could best be described as ultra-sweet.

"The hell you don't," McAllister shot back. "What the hell is going on here?"

"Moran doesn't like cursing, or blasphemy. He'd be very upset if I told him you were taking the Lord's name in vain right in the office."

"I didn't say anything about God," McAllister retorted, "and you haven't answered my question. What the hell is going on here?"

"Moran will believe anything I tell him, and if you swear at me again, I'll tell him you swore against God right here in the office. More than once, too!"

McAllister realized the conversation was going nowhere and spun on his heel, heading for the door. He could swear he heard Lemming chuckling to herself as he headed out to the parking lot.

The Hypocrite

He drove home in a daze, and did his best to keep his eyes on the heavy traffic. Before he knew it he was at Exit 16 on Rte. 2, and in a matter of seconds after exiting the highway was buried in the eastern Connecticut countryside. A few more minutes and he was pulling into the driveway of his home.

McAllister walked inside with the tread of a man who has major troubles and doesn't know what to do about them.

Inside Julia appeared from the kitchen, took one look at his face and asked, "What's wrong? Did we get the loan?"

He nodded in the affirmative, and handed her the envelope containing the papers and the check.

"Can you fix me a drink?" he asked.

"Sure," Julia answered, with a worried look on her face.

She walked back into the kitchen with McAllister right behind her, took a drink glass from the cupboard and pushed it under the refrigerator's ice dispenser. Three ice cubes dropped into the glass and Julia reached into the liquor cabinet.

"Dewars?" she asked.

"Glenmorangie," he responded.

"Really?" Julia asked as she reached to the back of the cabinet and took out a $100 bottle of eighteen-year-old scotch—the good stuff that was brought out for special occasions.

She poured enough scotch into the glass to float the ice cubes then handed it to her husband.

McAllister took a sip, savored it for a minute then looked at Julia. "Sit down, Hon," he told her. "You're not going to believe most of this, but I have to tell you, I have had one hell of a day."

Chapter 4

First Strike
Phone Tapping: What You Get for Missing Lunch
★ ★ ★

"I'm telling you it was the strangest thing I've ever experienced in the workplace! I have never seen or been involved in anything like this."

Bruce McAllister was taking a coffee break and talking quietly to his wife Julia on the phone. It was 10:30 a.m., Friday, the day after he missed the prayer luncheon in favor of signing a loan consolidation at the bank.

To McAllister, it was just a scheduling issue. No one mentioned the luncheon to him until just before noon the previous day, and upon reflection, he probably would have joined the elders of Moran Smythe's church if he could have. But since his work on refinancing their debts took nearly two months of his time, he was loathe to reschedule the closing even though it was scheduled for the same time as the luncheon.

More to the point, no one told him that the purpose of the luncheon was business, not prayer. Experience told him that the meeting probably would have started with a prayer and ended with a prayer, but in between the discussion was to be about business, or so he was

The Hypocrite

led to believe. However, he really hadn't expected the reception that was waiting for him when he returned from the bank the previous day, and the coldness that continued this morning.

He was relaying to Julia how Smythe barely acknowledged him that morning, and how he entered the building to a cold stare from Lemming. But after a question from Julia on his reaction to their childishness, he said, "I decided to out-Christian the Christians."

"Meaning what, exactly?" Julia responded.

"Meaning, if you are a real Christian you are supposed to be forgiving, non-manipulative. You are supposed to be helpful and try to get along with your fellow man, not try to trip him up at every twist and turn. All I did yesterday was keep an appointment at the bank, on my lunch hour, that was crucially important to us and our future.

"I didn't take any time away from work, I didn't leave the firm in the lurch. I just went to the bank and signed some papers so we could get our finances in order. No one told me about wanting me at lunch until just before lunch and even then it was never pointed out that it was supposed to be a business meeting not the regular prayer luncheon.

"Any normal person would be hell-bent on revenge for what went on here yesterday, but I just acted my usual pleasant self," McAllister concluded.

Julia laughed at that one. "Your usual pleasant self could scare an ogre sometimes."

"Well, I tried very hard to keep the ogre in the dungeon, and only my good side was allowed out to play," he responded.

"Good boy," Julia shot back. "Try to play nice and don't get dirty before you come in for dinner."

"I gotta go," McAllister said, ending the pleasantries. "Do you

The Hypocrite

want me to pick up anything on the way home?"

"No, we're good," Julia answered. "I'll see you later."

McAllister said goodbye and was about to hang up the phone, but he had wrapped the cord around a cup on his desk that held an assortment of pens and pencils, plus a letter opener. Still cradling the phone between his neck and shoulder as he unwrapped the cord, he heard the click as Julia hung up on her end, and then, an instant before the dial tone sounded, he heard another sound.

It was soft, but it was nonetheless clear, another "click!" Someone, somewhere in the building, was listening in on his conversation!

Whoever it was had misjudged his actions. Had McAllister not taken a few seconds to unwind his phone cord he would have hung up at roughly the same time as Julia and he would not have heard the interloper hanging up the extension.

McAllister deliberately banged the receiver down and jumped from his seat, striding purposely to Smythe's office. He entered without stopping, looking right and left for Moran, but the office was empty.

McAllister quickly did an about face and headed downstairs. He traversed the staircase in mere seconds and encountered a flustered looking Lemming sitting at her desk.

"What was that noise upstairs?" Lemming asked, with an unsuccessful effort to look nonchalant.

"What noise?" McAllister shot back.

"A bang. I heard a bang, like someone slammed down a phone!" Lemming was getting insistent but McAllister gave her no room to maneuver.

"I didn't hear anything," he replied with a straight face. "Maybe it was Moran."

"He isn't here. He's been gone for most of the morning," Lem-

The Hypocrite

ming averred with a smug "gotcha" look on her face.

"Really," McAllister replied. He had the information he needed now and without another word he abruptly returned to his office. Lemming glared at him behind his back, and McAllister could literally feel her gaze boring into him, but he didn't care.

Entering his office McAllister sat down, put his hands on the desk calendar in front of him—which always was a few months off because he just used it for taking notes when he was on the phone—and stared at nothing. He appeared to be in a trance, but McAllister's mind was racing, going over what had happened, and what he should do about it.

He experienced a few uncomfortable seconds as he reviewed the conversation with his wife, wondering if he said anything that would jeopardize his job. That was quickly replaced with unfocused anger, partly toward himself for worrying about what was or wasn't said, but mostly at Lemming for being a total jerk and at Smythe for allowing that kind of activity to exist unchecked in his business.

It was very quiet on the second floor of Smythe Partners for the rest of the morning, but oddly enough, it was quiet throughout the rest of the building too. Even though he was separated from the other workers by a ceiling and at least one wall, McAllister could occasionally hear laughter or snippets of conversations in other parts of the office when the door to the back was opened.

But not this morning. There was no sound anywhere. Lemming's phone didn't ring, there were no doors opening and closing, there was no conversation. It seemed as if the building was holding its breath, waiting for another shoe to drop, waiting for the next chapter in the ongoing drama that was the hallmark of employment at Smythe Partners Ltd.

Moran Smythe was not in the building and McAllister couldn't

The Hypocrite

remember hearing him leave before he made the call to his wife. As he reflected on the conversation McAllister realized that the one comment he made that could and likely would come back to haunt him was his revelation that his response to the earlier freeze-out from Lemming and Smythe was to "out-Christian the Christians."

Smythe hardly fit the mold of what McAllister considered a true Christian, but Smythe also made the point repeatedly that he considered himself to be the ultimate messenger of the word of God through his son Jesus Christ. No one should ever challenge him on that point or there would be hell to pay.

McAllister reflected on that for a few moments and digging into his recent memory realized that he even heard angry words coming from the conference room on occasion when Smythe and the elders held their weekly prayer luncheon. It seemed odd at the time as he never saw any of his other Christian friends get so worked up at similar meetings he attended.

Disagreements, or more appropriately, debates on the meaning of portions of scripture were not only common, but probably healthy for people who—if they were honest with themselves and each other—would have questions about the meanings of various passages in the Bible, many of which were written thousands of years earlier. Not only were these passages extraordinarily old, which wouldn't necessarily negate the original meaning, intent or relevance to the human condition, but they also were originally written in languages that died out long ago.

Even those that still existed had changed to such a degree that according to recent news reports it was taking a squad of highly trained linguists years to translate the Bible, one chapter at a time. Progress was so slow, it was reported, that a full translation from the original writings into modern languages, particularly English, would

The Hypocrite

not be accomplished in the lifetimes of some of the researchers.

McAllister was aware of these efforts to bring ancient writings into modern context, and he also was aware that many of the Biblical stories he learned in Sunday school many years earlier, particularly of the many miracles, might not have occurred exactly as they were related. That really didn't concern McAllister as he long ago concluded that his definition of a miracle didn't necessarily agree with the ancient definition of a miracle.

But while that didn't matter much to McAllister it obviously mattered greatly to Moran Smythe. In fact, McAllister learned quickly that if someone had a different slant on a Biblical matter than Smythe, and that included those who read versions of the Bible other than the King James version that Smythe favored, they were invariably wrong and he was invariably right, and Smythe never hesitated to say so.

Yet here was the self-professed ultimate Christian evangelist, acting in a decidedly un-Christian manner by wielding his presumed power over those who worked for him, and of special note, even those members of his own church, who presumably would share his views. The occasional outbursts from the conference room at lunch time taken in McAllister's current frame of mind appeared to be proof that Moran Smythe was a bully, not just in physical activities but also in mental and religious matters.

It was apparent that Smythe's forceful behavior in the office was carried on throughout his other activities, including his church.

But none of this explained why the previous day's luncheon was so important and why it was considered necessary for McAllister to be there. Lemming obviously knew, and used her information as well as her influence with Smythe to throw a monkey wrench into the works.

That may have worked for her personal vendettas, but it could

The Hypocrite

not have been a good thing for the business. Among all the other obvious and not-so-obvious facets of employment at Smythe Partners Ltd., the most glaringly obvious negative facet was Lemming's behavior.

She caused the termination of several employees, all of whom, according to those workers who knew them, were good at their jobs and had done nothing to deserve their fates, other than to tick off Lemming. But Smythe, if he was even a fraction as smart as he considered himself to be, would have and certainly should have seen the pattern develop.

A tiff between the worker and Lemming would invariably be followed by computer issues that resulted in lost or ruined projects that had to be resurrected from scratch. This took additional time, often considerable additional time, that had to negatively affect the bottom line.

Smythe usually had to bid on contracts to take on or keep clients, as did most businesses, and the figures he used in preparing those bids were based on a certain amount of time devoted to each phase of the project. Doubling the time it took to complete any phase twice would correspondingly reduce the ultimate profit to the company—in addition to skewing the deadlines under which each department operated.

If that happened often enough there would be no more company. Smythe had to know that. He couldn't have built a company that could be considered successful without knowing how the departments were interrelated and how repeated conflicts in any or all of them could bring down the entire firm.

Yet he continued to side with Lemming, allowing her to create false dramas, and use her access to the computer system to tinker with other people's work, to the point of destroying it.

The Hypocrite

McAllister sat at his desk in deep reverie for more than an hour. He was vaguely conscious of the unusual quiet in the building and at some point he realized that his desk calendar was still on May even though it was nearly August. He made a mental note to update it soon, also knowing full well that it wouldn't happen until he ran out of room for notes on the current page, or spilled coffee on it.

Eventually he glanced at the clock on the wall and realized it was nearly noon. He decided to go out for lunch even though Julia had packed one for him—a tuna salad sandwich, chips, apple and carton of juice. It would be good, he knew from experience, but, for reasons he didn't understand, it suddenly was not what he wanted.

McAllister walked downstairs and found himself in an empty reception room. He thought he heard a door closing when he stood up from his desk, scraping his chair on the floor, and deduced it was Lemming leaving her work station. He actually was relieved that he didn't have to put up with her perversions today.

He climbed into his truck and headed out the driveway, remembering at the last minute that, despite the uproar the previous day, he was successful in convincing Moran Smythe to write "Bruce McAllister is employed at Smythe Partners Ltd." across a piece of paper bearing the company's logo. He even signed it.

McAllister left it on the seat of his truck when he arrived at work that morning and noticed it as he was leaving. He pulled over to the side of the driveway, in what Julia would have told him was a fit of paranoia, and pulled the letter from its folder. He scanned it again just to make sure it hadn't been tampered with, and satisfied, put it back and headed to the bank.

It took only a minute to drop the letter off for the manager's perusal and then he was back in the truck. He partly retraced his route back to Parsonage Street, but upon reaching the intersection with

The Hypocrite

Old Main Street, McAllister turned left, heading toward Wethersfield.

Old Main Street continued under the highway and turned into Middletown Avenue at the town line. He followed that street until he reached Wells Road and turned right which took him into the heart of Old Wethersfield.

Within a few blocks McAllister was nearly to Wethersfield Cove, where he sometimes ate lunch. But well before that he passed a very old tavern on his right and a seed company on his left, then at the next block pulled into a parking space in front of a small deli.

He walked inside, was recognized by the lady behind the counter who greeted him and took his order—a pastrami sandwich with mustard on rye bread and a homemade dill pickle. Although he rarely drank coffee in the afternoon he ordered a small container of one of the special brews, paid and took his bag back to the truck.

McAllister nearly headed for the cove, but it often was crowded there and he decided instead to eat lunch in the nearby cemetery which usually had far fewer people around. He did that once in a while too, and was never bothered there. He guessed that people just automatically assumed that if you were parked in a cemetery and weren't causing any problems that you were visiting the dead.

He went to the rear of the parcel where there was still room for new graves, behind a church, but south of the really, really old section of the graveyard. He parked on the grass under a huge old oak tree facing back toward the entrance, and slowly ate his lunch. It was pleasant there and quiet. Birds were chirping in the tree above him, which offered plentiful shade, and he heard the occasional hum of insects.

The day was sunny, the sky achingly blue, but the temperature was only in the mid-seventies and the humidity was low. It was peace-

The Hypocrite

ful and quiet, just what McAllister needed.

He was sorry for not eating the lunch Julia packed for him, but he knew she would understand. Today he just wanted to give himself a bit of a treat, to relax a bit and remind himself why he was working in a literal hell hole of small minds and pettiness, when he really wanted to get started on rebuilding his own business.

If he had any regrets it was only that he seemed to have incurred the wrath of the elders, apparently because they didn't know what really transpired the previous day. McAllister did like them and was sure he would have enjoyed their company, but due to Lemming's manipulations they now were obviously suffering from a serious case of hurt feelings.

But again, he was left wondering what it was that convinced Smythe to take her word over the word of anyone who spoke against her. From what McAllister could see after a limited time employed there, she was a troublemaker and no matter who complained about her, she was the one person who was always at the center of things.

It should have been obvious what she was doing. It was obvious what she was doing, yet Smythe tolerated it. Why?

McAllister finished his lunch and sat listening to the radio, tuned to the local Hartford oldies station at a decibel level just barely above audible. He inherited that habit from his father, listening to the oldies station that is, and remembered bantering with him when a song came on that seemed to have no redeeming value of any kind.

"I didn't like it when it came out and I don't like it now," his father would respond. "But someone must have, because for a few weeks way back when, they played that damn song every time I turned on the radio. Somebody must have been paid a ton of money to play that junk."

Today there were only good songs, of the kind that McAllister

The Hypocrite

remembered from his youth when his father would take him along on a ride. It was calming, and even produced a few minutes of true nostalgia, remembering a time when things certainly seemed to be better than they were today.

McAllister sat staring out the driver's window, but looking at nothing actually. He could see right to the front of the cemetery and across the street to the old tavern's parking lot. That sight line would be a factor in a few months, but he didn't realize it then, even though he was unconsciously making a mental note of his surroundings.

If he thought about it at all, McAllister probably would have laughed to himself, thinking that becoming familiar with your surroundings is something "big, tough Marines" do even when they're off duty and no longer in uniform.

Eventually a lone male figure came into his view and for a second McAllister ignored the other presence, assuming correctly that it was a mourner, coming to visit the grave of a loved one. But as the man grew closer McAllister refocused on him and realized the long, lean form of none other than Derrick Simpson, the elder.

Simpson must have recognized McAllister's truck because he was on a beeline for it. McAllister smiled as he grew close enough for facial recognition but Simpson responded only with a curt nod.

"Odd seeing you here," Simpson said by way of greeting.

"I come here for lunch when I need a mental vacation," McAllister responded. "Some days this is the perfect spot to get away from it all."

Simpson didn't respond to that but went straight to his point. "We really missed you at lunch yesterday. The other elders are quite upset. They wanted your input on a matter that is of utmost importance to our church, and Moran assured us you would be there. They feel disrespected, and frankly, so do I."

The Hypocrite

"Well, I understand why you'd be upset if you were told I was coming, but you should know that I wasn't informed that it was a business luncheon or that my presence was required. I thought it was the regular prayer luncheon, and I actually thought I'd stop in and say hello if I could get back in time.

"But I have been working on those banking issues I told you about for a couple of months now, and it meant the world to my wife that I was able to close on the loan consolidation. If someone had told me the nature of the meeting beforehand, I could have scheduled the closing at another time, even taken an hour off at another part of the day if necessary."

Simpson said nothing for a minute, but the set of his jaw showed that he was struggling internally with a weighty issue. Finally he sighed and said with some resignation, "Are you aware that Gail Lemming told us she personally informed you earlier in the week that your work schedule would have to be rearranged for Thursday? Did you know that she said you confirmed your attendance to her and then suddenly changed your plans at the last minute?"

"Nothing of the kind happened," McAllister replied. "She showed up at my office door a few minutes before noon and said I was invited to the luncheon. I explained that I had another appointment that I couldn't change and offered to explain it to Moran.

"But oddly enough, he wasn't in his office or anywhere in the building when I went looking for him. That was just before I saw you out on the sidewalk."

Simpson stood quietly for a few seconds, and then asked, "Why do you say it was odd that Moran wasn't around?"

"Because I never heard Lemming coming up the stairs before she appeared at my office door. She can't come up those steps quietly, if you get my drift, but I never heard her, meaning she was in Moran's

The Hypocrite

office before she came to my office. But I heard Moran leave nearly a half-hour earlier, so I have no idea what she was up to."

Simpson again paused, and then asked quietly, "She was up in Moran's office but stayed there after he left? Does that occur often?"

"Not really," McAllister responded. "Like I said, she has a hard time navigating those steps, so she only comes up on occasion and when she does it is quite the occasion, no pun intended."

Simpson nodded, and then suddenly changed the subject to more mundane issues. He chatted for a bit, then said he was off to visit his late wife's grave. They said their good-byes and Simpson walked toward the east side of the cemetery as McAllister resumed listening to the oldies station.

Finally it was getting uncomfortably close to 1 p.m., and he reluctantly started the truck and left the cemetery. He took a right at the entrance, located across from the tavern, and then made a left at the intersection retracing his route back into Rocky Hill.

There was no reason to take notice of what anyone else was doing at that time, but within seconds of McAllister's leaving the cemetery, a dark sedan pulled out from the tavern parking lot and began shadowing him. McAllister wouldn't have recognized the car, even if he took notice of it, since it was parked deep in the rear of the lot, in the shade of the nearby trees.

Old Main Street was a two-lane street that ran parallel to the six-lane Silas Dean Highway, but it had a country look to it, few traffic lights, lots of shade trees alongside and there was far less traffic. McAllister was vaguely aware of other vehicles behind him, but never connected with the dark sedan. It took up a position several cars behind him and the driver did nothing that would call attention to himself.

McAllister made good time, arriving back at the office a few

The Hypocrite

minutes before 1 p.m. When he pulled into the parking lot, the sedan sped up, heading down the street.

Feeling a bit aggressive McAllister walked quickly but quietly to the main door and opened it abruptly, there finding Smythe and Lemming in what appeared to be a very deep discussion.

Lemming was seated at her workstation and Smythe was on her side of the desk, bent over talking in a very low voice. They both jumped as he entered and quickly put a few feet of space between them. Smythe bore an irritated look and McAllister anticipated another onslaught from him, similar to his commentary—or inquisition—from the previous day.

Instead, Smythe quickly covered up his true feelings, pasting a smile across his face and saying with fake heartiness, "Ah, McAllister, right on time! How was lunch?"

"Lunch was fine," McAllister responded, very much on his guard.

"Did you go to a restaurant, or a fast food place?" Smythe continued, with excessive friendliness.

"No, I just went to a deli over in the center of Old Wethersfield. I got a sandwich and ate it under a tree in the Village Cemetery. It was very peaceful there."

By now McAllister was getting anxious to finish this drivel and escape to his office, but Smythe wasn't done.

"Well, we all need a little peace every so often. It's good for the heart and good for the soul. It refreshes us and gives us the energy to face each day with hope and anticipation."

He sounded exactly as if he were speaking to the congregation at his church, and McAllister had the definite impression that Smythe was sermonizing.

"It certainly does," he responded, edging toward the staircase.

The Hypocrite

"You know, my ancestors helped settle Wethersfield," Smythe asserted with obvious pride of ownership. "Original founders of the colony, they were. Pillars of the community. Successful in business, in the church, in government. Good stock. Good stock."

Smythe was positively beaming by now and as he caught his breath, McAllister nodded, turned on his heel and started up the staircase. He could have looked back down to see if they had resumed their semi-private tête-à-tête but McAllister fought the impulse and continued into his office without looking back.

The remainder of his day was a near mirror image of his morning, with McAllister spending more time staring at his desk calendar than working, although he did make some desultory efforts to complete a project that was nearing deadline.

When he came upstairs a good half-hour after McAllister returned from lunch, Smythe stuck his head in the door briefly to say, "Just seeing how you're doing." A couple of hours later, he also stuck his head in the door to say he was leaving, which came as a complete surprise to McAllister.

At quitting time he made sure, as he did every night, to save all of his files to a flash drive, a routine that now took on more importance than ever. This time he also pocketed the flash drive instead of putting it in his desk drawer, perhaps unnecessarily but a precaution he preferred to deal with, knowing that Lemming was on the warpath and there was no limit to her viciousness.

Lemming's workstation was vacant and there were no sounds coming from the rest of the building as he exited the front door. McAllister got in the truck, left the property and took the usual route home.

He pulled into his driveway and walked in the door, still shaking his head at the weirdness of his day.

The Hypocrite

Julia walked out of the kitchen, took one look at his face, and said simply, "Scotch?"

McAllister looked at her for a few seconds, and then shook his head no.

"I think an ice-water would be great."

Julia went to the cupboard and took down a tumbler, moving to the fridge where she pushed it under the ice maker and filling it with crushed ice. Pouring tap water into the ice she handed the full glass to her husband.

He sipped, then gulped, said, "Ahhh," with false satisfaction, turned on his heel and headed off to change into his exercise clothes.

Chapter 5

Tower of Babel
(Tripping with the Virgin Mary)

"I'm not saying Jesus didn't have a mother and I'm not saying that the mother he did have was not a special person.

"What I am saying is, simply, that there is evidence that the story of the Virgin Mary didn't show up until considerably after the death of Jesus. And, it is altogether possible, given the political climate of the time, that the Virgin Birth story was manufactured to give the Christians a sense of mysticism to offset the immortality claims of the Roman Emperor."

McAllister was riding in Smythe's car, a late model Lexus, on the way to a client meeting, and found himself in the unenviable position of defending his part in a conversation that had predictably deteriorated into tension bordering on hostility. Smythe took his usual know-it-all attitude regarding matters of religion, especially the Christian religion, after McAllister made what he considered to be a relatively benign observation.

In the current discussion, McAllister remarked that he was reading a lot about the history of Biblical times, and had come across

The Hypocrite

some research indicating that Mary, mother of Jesus Christ, was not mentioned as having given Virgin Birth until well after Christ died. Some researchers suspected that the early Christians may have believed they needed a more mystical approach to their new-found religion, especially since the Roman Emperors claimed they were descended from both Gods and man.

"Debunker!" Smythe shouted. "Debunker!" again with a voice so strained that it nearly cracked. "You are one of them," he sneered. "They think there is no God, they think this was all just some cosmic accident waiting to happen. They do everything they can to slur the name of the Almighty and undermine his work, and the work of his loyal subjects here on earth."

"I'm no such thing, Moran," McAllister responded, with what Smythe took as an aggravating calmness. "I'm merely pointing out that research into the lives of the people who knew Christ when he lived indicates that—given the relative lack of information on science, medicine and other evolving fields of knowledge at the time—it wouldn't be unheard of to create a more mystical and therefore sympathetic character. Remember, the Christian God had to offset a host of pagan deities.

"Besides," McAllister continued, "I first heard the story that Moses led the Israelites out of Egypt across the Sea of Reeds rather than the Red Sea, from a Christian evangelist, and he had no reason to say otherwise. In fact, I think that virtually every miracle I read or heard about from Biblical times encompassed a series of minor miracles that people of the time then added up to one big miracle, but frankly, they needed no extra boost to lock in my sense of belief.

"I find it far more likely that Moses fooled the Egyptian army, keeping their archers with their heavy chariots at bay long enough for the Jews to escape to the Sinai, than to believe in a Charlton Heston

The Hypocrite

lookalike standing on a rock with flowing robes and long hair and beard pointing a stick at the Red Sea and making it part long enough to cross it.

"In fact, if Moses had the power to part the Red Sea, he didn't even have to go there to do it. I figure he could have sat in a tent someplace and left tracks up to the edge of the water and waited for the Egyptians to try to get across. Then, whammo, pull the plug and let them drown. Then he could have gone back into Egypt and conquered the whole place while it was undefended." McAllister was going beyond the norm, and much further than was necessary, but he was enjoying himself in a perverse sort of way.

"Either way it was a miraculous occurrence no matter which version you believe. I don't need hocus-pocus for me to believe a miracle occurred."

It was now mid-October and in the months since he began working at Smythe Partners, McAllister heard "the one and only" version of the Bible so often that it was becoming like background music. There was but one version according to Moran Smythe and that version was his and his alone. And you had better keep it to yourself if you had any alternative viewpoints.

McAllister even noted to Julia on occasion that he heard the elders raise their voices when they came for their Thursday luncheons and Bible study classes and ran into the Word According to Smythe. It was a recurring theme with McAllister because he had never encountered anyone who was so myopic and so determined to force his view on everyone else, even people who were just trying to reason their way through ancient parables and connect them to modern issues.

The truth was, there was plenty of room in the Bible for discussion, debate and interpretation. That was one of the great attractions

The Hypocrite

of the Bible and a considerable lure for people who had questions or points of view.

In fact, McAllister occasionally opined that there were nearly as many versions of the Bible as interpretations of Biblical events.

McAllister gave it one last shot, and promised himself he would relate this to Julia at the end of what quickly was becoming another in a very long string of very long days. "I don't know," he said, "given the lack of verification at the time of Jesus' birth, I wonder if someday four-hundred years from now someone is going to say that David Copperfield is the new messiah because he made Niagara Falls disappear on television."

It was all he could do to keep from laughing out loud—at first—but Smythe took care of that right away.

"Debunker!" Smythe shouted again. "There will be no more of this talk in my car on my time in my company while I am paying you a salary that exists solely because of my work, which exists thanks to the Lord Almighty and his son, my Savior, Jesus Christ!"

At that McAllister finally stopped talking. He regretted going too far, but there were times when Smythe was so smug, so self-important, so insulting and so abusive that McAllister couldn't help but respond. Nonetheless, he reminded himself that his job still depended on Moran Smythe's good will, or at least his needs of the moment.

McAllister wasn't overly worried about his value to the company. In fact he was going on this client call with Smythe because Smythe wanted him to start working on a list of potential new clients that McAllister was to compile. These would be the government contracts that McAllister spoke of back when he interviewed for the job.

Smythe wanted to see how McAllister handled pitching potential clients, and when he was satisfied that McAllister was competent in that area, they would start working on much bigger contracts with

The Hypocrite

the feds.

However, McAllister realized soon after he started work at the company that Moran Smythe was a complete fraud, fake and flake. Should Smythe become overly agitated and forget his real reason for hiring McAllister, he and Julia would find themselves right back where they were at the beginning of the year.

So, he enjoyed the scenery, especially the colorful fall leaves, as Smythe drove first to Hartford then east on Interstate 84. They were going to visit a potential client in Union, Connecticut, a small town on the east of the state bordering Massachusetts. It was a long drive and the silence should give Smythe time to get his blood pressure under control—but it didn't.

He muttered to himself on occasion, as much to relieve his own tension as to let McAllister know he was still upset with the direction of their earlier conversation. Smythe did not like to be contradicted. In fact, he hated to be contradicted and he could feel the red hot response of blood rushing to his head whenever he was challenged as he was this morning.

Unfortunately, when Smythe got angry while he was behind the wheel he responded accordingly, with extra pressure on the gas pedal and an increased intolerance of anyone else on the road. He became enraged at minor inconveniences such as slower drivers ahead of him who had the temerity to pass another vehicle at a mere ten miles per hour over the speed limit. His anger became volcanic if they then stayed in the passing lane too long for Smythe's liking, or prevented him from blasting past both vehicles with what could only be described as a sense of superiority.

Smythe would ride right up on the offending vehicle's bumper, flashing his lights and blowing his horn to show that he was King of the Road and everyone else should make way for His Majesty. McAl-

The Hypocrite

lister twice checked to make sure his seat belt was securely fastened and found himself surreptitiously looking over at Smythe's speedometer to see how fast they were going. The needle pretty much stayed well above eighty miles per hour, and more often than not was close to ninety.

If Smythe made the trip up I-84 to Union more often, he would know that the Connecticut State Police run a regular speed trap on that section of the highway, often manned by a trooper who has a reputation as impossible to challenge—or reason with—when he nabs an offending driver.

Other troopers would laugh when describing his habit of walking right out into traffic, pointing at the chosen driver, and motioning that he was reeling them in like a fish on a line. "He'd give his grandmother a ticket if she was one mile over the speed limit," his colleagues would often remark.

As luck would have it—if you believe in luck—the Super Trooper was on duty that day and had just finished a coffee break when his dashboard radar unit lit up like a Christmas tree. West of him about a quarter of a mile, Smythe finally forced another car to yield to his demands and as the other driver returned to the slower lane, Smythe floored it, hitting above the ninety mile per hour mark in a move that literally had McAllister holding on to the door armrest with a white-knuckle grip.

They saw the trooper at the same time, with Smythe shouting an expletive and McAllister looking skyward and silently mouthing, "Thank you, God."

The trooper was already out of his cruiser, which probably saved Smythe from a worse fate, making his "reeling them in" motion and pointing directly at Smythe. "You," he shouted. "Pull over!"

The veins on Smythe's head threatened to burst, and McAllis-

The Hypocrite

ter thought that Smythe was considering making a run for the border. But a few hundred yards ahead, another trooper was waiting in a chase cruiser for just those moments. The state police had this one covered and Smythe had no choice but to pull alongside the guardrail.

Smythe's muttering increased in speed and volume, and McAllister had the sinking sensation that this was going to deteriorate into one of those do–you-know-who-I-am? moments. "How dare you pull me over? I am an important person, on important business and you not only are a piss-ant you are delaying me!"

The trooper walked alongside Smythe's Lexus with his hand on his pistol grip looking into the back seat, then bending down to face Smythe directly, simultaneously giving McAllister the once over. "Hands on the dashboard," he ordered, and McAllister instantly complied.

McAllister had quite a few friends in law enforcement and many of them related to him the tension that accompanies the first minutes of a pending arrest, even if it is just a traffic issue. They never knew what or who they would encounter and the best thing the offender can do is comply with their orders until the situation is resolved.

"My hands are already on the wheel," Smythe responded, attempting to gain dominance over the situation.

"Here we go," McAllister thought to himself.

"I said hands on the dashboard," the trooper barked. His face took on the countenance of granite and his voice became even harder, if that was possible.

"Do it now or I'll put you on the ground in cuffs!"

Smythe did as ordered but with just a hint of slowness to show that he wasn't cowed by the trooper.

"Are you carrying a weapon?"

The Hypocrite

Smythe looked like he was stung by a bee. "No," he answered abruptly.

"Are there any weapons in the vehicle?"

"No."

"Where are your license and registration?" the trooper asked, his voice still cold and hard.

Smythe looked at the trooper with a half-smile and responded with a cloying sweetness that sounded exactly like Lemming when she was playing office politics, "Why they're in my wallet, in my right rear trousers pocket, Trooper." He used the word "trooper" as others would use an expletive, and that didn't go unnoticed by the officer.

"Using your right hand and only your right hand, reach slowly back and remove your wallet."

Smythe did as ordered, and the trooper further instructed, "Remove your license, registration and insurance card, using both hands. Do it slowly. Hand them to me and then put your wallet and your hands back on the dash."

Smythe did as ordered and the trooper took the documents. He turned to walk back to his cruiser to run the license and other IDs, but not before admonishing Smythe, "Keep your hands on the dash, and don't move!"

McAllister took it all in silently. He kept his hands on the dash and looked straight ahead, not offering either challenge or threat to the trooper. But using his peripheral vision he could see Smythe's body language and it was communicating hostility.

After a few minutes the trooper returned. He appeared to be a bit relaxed, but McAllister was taking no chances. He hadn't moved since the first order and he stayed that way until the trooper told him, "You both can relax now."

McAllister sat back then and quietly enjoyed the rest of the

The Hypocrite

show.

"Mr. Smythe, I clocked you doing eighty-eight miles per hour in a sixty-five mile per hour zone. I have the feeling that you actually went faster after my radar locked on but I guess today is your lucky day. The fine for this offense will run you several hundred dollars and is spelled out on the back of this ticket. You can either mail in the fine or challenge it in court. If you do that the court will respond with a time, date and place where you can appear to argue your case."

The trooper stopped for a few seconds to let it all sink in, then said with a half-smile, "I go to court two or three times a month to deal with wise guys who think they can beat the system. I consider it my civic duty. And I never lose.

"Now, Mr. Smythe, just so I have another story for my collection to tell back at the barracks this afternoon, why were you in such a hurry?"

Smythe choked back a retort and replied, "I'm late for a business appointment. The economy stinks and I'm trying to keep my business afloat. I didn't want to show up late but the traffic back in Hartford was slow due to an accident. I was just trying to make up for lost time."

The trooper just nodded and straightened up. McAllister was a bit impressed that some of what Smythe told the trooper was true—except that there was no traffic backup, they weren't late, the meeting was still a half-hour off and they were only a few minutes away from the potential client's company.

Everything else was true though.

The trooper moved as though he was going to return to his cruiser but then did something that neither Smythe nor McAllister expected. He turned, walked around the front of the Lexus and using a ring on his right hand tapped on McAllister's window, telling him

The Hypocrite

at the same time, "Roll this down."

McAllister did as instructed and the trooper leaned down, asking, "What's your status in life?"

"I work for him," McAllister replied. "When we get hired I have to figure out ways to get clients' messages to the public."

"Do you go on these trips with him all the time?"

"Not really," McAllister replied. "Just when my input is needed."

"You might want to consider driving your own car from now on," the trooper admonished. "We usually end up scraping guys like him off the road. Have a good day."

The trooper returned to Smythe's window and leaned down one last time. "Your speed today was two miles off a reckless driving charge. If you had been going over ninety I could arrest you and impound your car. Remember that the next time you think the speed limits are for everyone except you."

"Have a nice day," he said again and returned to his cruiser.

For about three minutes Smythe was the model of a good driver, checking his mirrors, checking the oncoming vehicles, putting his blinker on before accelerating and moving into the flow of traffic. But the instant he was out of sight of the chase vehicle he took the ticket from the dash and tried to throw it in McAllister's face!

"See what happened because of you? See what you caused? See what you made me do? You just cost me hundreds of dollars!"

His face was literally a mottled purple color and McAllister briefly worried that Smythe might have a stroke before they even got to their meeting. McAllister fought back an urge to jump ugly all over Smythe.

Smythe's driving habits were not the result of McAllister's questioning regardless of how persistent he was in raising issues that angered Smythe. His driving habits were instead a reflection of Smythe's

The Hypocrite

basic view of the universe. He was at its center, all else revolved around him and anything that got in his way was to be removed by whatever means he favored at the moment.

His decision to drive like a maniac because he couldn't crush McAllister's point of view was his and his alone and the resultant ticket was his penalty, not McAllister's. Naturally, Moran Smythe didn't see it that way.

As if to mock him further, the ticket he attempted to toss into McAllister's face as a sort of exclamation point to his anger, got caught in an air current inside the car—McAllister still had his window open, and it blew right back at Smythe. For an instant it appeared to hang in a hover and then slid dangerously close to McAllister's open window before finally blowing into the back seat and coming to rest on the floor.

McAllister didn't even want to think what Smythe would have done if the ticket blew out of his window.

Fortunately, the client's business was just off the highway and exit 74 was just ahead of them. Smythe tried to bring himself under control while McAllister sat, outwardly calm but inwardly just about lethal.

After he returned from combat and had some time to put things into perspective, McAllister sat down with Julia, telling her that for the rest of his life there always would be a question in his mind about his future actions. Would there be a time and place when something so heinous occurred that he would again be capable of killing?

The simple answer, he told her, was yes, he could and he would.

But he also reassured her that despite the media portrayals of combat veterans that went back for generations, he never lost a minute of sleep, nor did he endure flashbacks to his times in the Marines, except for the occasional nightmare where he was back in recruit

The Hypocrite

training at Parris Island. Anyone who has ever gone through Marine recruit training will understand that situation.

He knew without question that, if the lives of those he cared for were in danger, he could kill to save them as coldly and as calmly as he did in combat. But that wasn't the situation he questioned.

He wondered at times if he could maintain control if someone did something to him personally that would flip his internal control switch from "idle" to "kill."

Summing it up for Julia he said, "I go out of my way to appear calm, even acquiescent. But sometimes I just get that feeling, that look, and the person giving me crap doesn't realize that I am not looking at them, I'm looking through them as if their head was blown away by my fifty-caliber. I've met a lot of blowhards and wannabes since I came back, guys who either never went, or just dipped their toe in enough to say they'd been in, but didn't make the hard decisions.

"They always overcompensate. They always have the biggest stories, the most impossible stories, or think they have to one-up anyone who might just want to work through something. They never figure it out," he told Julia, "but I'll tell this to you and only to you. I am the only man in this world that I fear, not because there aren't people who are bigger or stronger or tougher, but because I know I can kill any one of them in an instant and they'll never know what's on my mind until it's too late.

"My fear about myself is that something will set me off and I won't be able to stop, then we'll suffer in the long run. That's why I try to keep things on an even keel as much as possible and people sometimes misunderstand me when I laugh at an insult or a slight. It's not that I give a rat's ass about them or how tough they are. It's just that I don't want to go back to that combat mentality and lose

The Hypocrite

everything we've built."

McAllister brought himself back to the present and, realizing that mentally he was treading on very, very dangerous ground, worked even harder to bring his emotions under control. Smythe had underestimated him, and that was a stupid thing to do. But Smythe was a stupid man and today that stupidity revealed itself glaringly.

Smythe pulled into a parking space and made a show of dragging his briefcase from the backseat to the front. He unsnapped it, took a cursory look inside then closed it—hard.

"Don't say anything unless I tell you to," he growled at McAllister. "I don't want you blowing this proposal."

That was a bit more than McAllister was willing to ignore, and with an icy voice and stare to match, he looked at Smythe, asking tersely, "Would you prefer me to sit here and wait for you?"

Once again Smythe underestimated the situation and snapped back, "Don't get smart with me, just do what you're told and keep your mouth shut!"

With that Smythe opened his door and McAllister followed suit. They walked toward the building entrance, neither saying a word, entering the building where they encountered the receptionist.

Smythe brusquely announced himself and gave the woman the name of his contact.

"Have a seat," she said with a pleasantness that was sorely missing at Smythe Partners. "He'll be right with you."

In just a minute, the plant manager, a no-nonsense looking man who obviously knew his way around a manufacturing facility, came through a set of swinging doors. He was tallish, maybe six feet or so, lean, and to McAllister's surprise had a full head of very white hair, appearing to be in his late seventies. McAllister had been to a few of these meetings and their contact usually was a person in his forties or

The Hypocrite

fifties tops.

"Mr. Smythe?" the manager inquired. Smythe nodded and extended his hand to shake it.

The manager took Smythe's hand firmly and introduced himself. "Jack Jamieson," he said.

Looking at McAllister, Jamieson asked, "And you are?"

Before McAllister could respond Smythe interrupted, "That's McAllister. He's my ad guy."

"Got a first name, McAllister?" Jamieson asked with a somewhat quizzical look.

"Bruce," McAllister responded before Smythe could stick his nose in again.

Jamieson nodded and turned back toward the door where he had entered the reception area. "Come with me," he said over his shoulder and took off with a stride that would seem normal on a man half his age.

They walked through a busy manufacturing area crammed with computerized machines, and yellow lines on the floor marking areas where they could walk. At the side of the main work area was a small conference room, big enough to hold a dozen people, but otherwise it was sparse, no frills.

Jamieson took a seat at the head of the conference table and motioned to Smythe and McAllister to join him.

"So what do you have for me?" Jamieson asked after they were settled.

Smythe cleared his throat, reached out to a pitcher of ice water in the center of the table, poured himself a glass and put it back without asking if anyone else was thirsty. McAllister noticed what he considered to be a social and business gaffe and had the distinct feeling that Jamieson noticed it too.

The Hypocrite

Smythe launched into his set routine, outlining his business, what it did, how it worked and what it could do for Jamieson's firm. He droned on in a monotone that showed he had worked to memorize the routine without truly having a passion for his message.

Jamieson stared at Smythe during most of the presentation, his face impassive, but occasionally looking over at McAllister, as if waiting for his part in the dog and pony show. But McAllister had no part, he was window dressing as far as Smythe was concerned, and Smythe hurried through his delivery so as to discourage interruptions or questions.

Finally, he was through and Jamieson looked at him for ten seconds or so in absolute silence.

Just as it began to get uncomfortable, he shifted in his chair, looked at McAllister and said quietly, "So, what do you do? What's your part in all of this?"

Once again, as McAllister was about to speak, Smythe cut in, "I already told you. He's my ad guy. He just does the words for the packages."

"I know what you told me," Jamieson responded coldly. "I want to hear from McAllister. What does he do, how does he do it, what has he accomplished in the past? He will produce the first thing my potential customers will see and I want to know if he has any idea how to convince them to pick up the product, look it over, see how it performs."

"Basically," McAllister responded, after shooting a hard glance at Smythe that wasn't missed by Jamieson, "I use my life experiences to figure what would make me want to look at the product further. Then I come up with some short quotes—sound bites the media calls them—that get people to want to hear or see more."

It felt good to have a chance to speak, but all the time he was

The Hypocrite

talking, Smythe was shooting daggers at McAllister with his eyes. McAllister felt it, and Jamieson saw it too.

Jamieson held up his hand for McAllister to stop, which he did, and then Jamieson picked up a nearby phone and dialed an internal extension. He spoke briefly and quietly and within seconds of the time he hung up, a worker entered the conference room.

He appeared to be in his forties, and if there is a picture of what a stereotypical engineer would look like, he fit the bill. He was fit, with a receding hairline, wire-rimmed glasses and a dress shirt, which, like Jamieson's, was open at the throat. He was wearing a tie but it, too, was loosened. McAllister would not have been surprised if there were an old-fashioned slide rule protruding from his pocket but that one facet of the stereotype was missing—probably replaced by a palm-sized pocket calculator.

"This is Tom Anderson," Jamieson said by way of introduction. "This place wouldn't be half of what it is without him. Tom, take Mr. Smythe for a tour of our facility so he can see what we do here. Try to be back in fifteen minutes. I have a few more questions for his associate. If we can do this at the same time I'll be able to make a decision before we finish up."

Smythe looked terribly perplexed, but stood, nonetheless, and he left the room following behind Anderson.

Jamieson looked at McAllister and inquired, "Do you always keep your hair that short?"

"Yes," McAllister replied without embellishing.

"Military?"

"Marines. Six years total active."

"Combat?"

"Yes," McAllister again replied, wondering why the conversation was going this way. "I was a fifty-caliber gunner on armored

The Hypocrite

troop carriers. Made the Iraq invasion, fought in Fallujah and then spent time out in Anbar Province."

"Machine gunner? How many bad guys did you kill?" The question from Jamieson seemed intrusive and way too familiar. McAllister was not at all comfortable with it. Nonetheless, he was there on business and there was something trustworthy about Jamieson.

"I have no idea," McAllister replied. "Lots of times they were hiding behind walls or buildings that I could shoot through with the fifty-caliber, but I didn't see what happened after the shooting stopped. Lots of other times there were so many of us shooting at once that it was impossible to figure who did what. There were enough times that I know I'm responsible for some, but I never got into that body count mentality."

Jamieson was looking straight at McAllister as he answered the question, and then after a short pause Jamieson said, "If you had answered that question any other way, I would not have hired you."

He then held out his hand again to shake and said simply "Semper Fi. Chosin Reservoir."

McAllister's jaw dropped and he managed to say in what was nearly a hoarse whisper, "The Frozen Chosin?"

Jamieson nodded.

McAllister, for one of the very few times in his life, was in awe, and speechless. Sitting at the table with him was a hero of one of the most difficult and misunderstood battles in the entire Marine Corps history.

In the first year of the Korean War from roughly November 6 to December 23, 1950, elements of the 1st Marine Division and Regimental Combat Teams from the 8th Army Division were sent on parallel courses into what had been North Korea, demolishing the Korean communists as they went. But the Chinese communists,

The Hypocrite

not that far away across the Yalu River, were secretly amassing their forces—estimated by some analysts to be a million soldiers—because they didn't trust the American General, Douglas MacArthur, to stop at the border.

The Chinese launched an unheard of human wave assault estimated to be 200,000 strong, against the American forces at the Chosin Reservoir, smashing through Army lines on the east, and surrounding the Marines on the west. The Army was ordered to retreat to Seoul, where under Gen. Matthew Ridgway they regrouped and rejoined the fight.

The Marines, and some survivors of the Army units, however, chose to fight their way out and headed toward the coastal city of Hungnam, nearly eighty miles away over some of the most unforgiving terrain in the world, in temperatures that at night reached as low as thirty degrees below zero or worse. Under Gen. Oliver Smith and reinforcements commanded by the famed Marine Col. Lewis "Chesty" Puller, the Marines and other UN troops effectively destroyed or crippled seven Chinese divisions which attempted to block their progress.

Marine losses in the campaign numbered 836 killed and thousands wounded. Many others suffered crippling frostbite. US Army losses numbered around 2,000 killed and 1,000 wounded. In the years since the battle at the Chosin, it has been difficult to ascertain exact Chinese losses, but they are estimated at 35,000 killed and at least three times that many wounded.

When the Marines successfully executed The Breakout, as it was called, some pundits attempted to portray the battle as a retreat and a defeat for the Marines. But, General Smith was quoted as saying, "Retreat? Hell, we are attacking in another direction!"

The Marine Generals and Navy Admirals wanted to establish

The Hypocrite

defensive positions at Hungnam and stay there throughout the winter for a renewed offensive in the spring, but political interference prevailed and they were forced to board ships and depart.

McAllister extended his hand, "Semper Fi," he said, nearly choking on emotion. "You're the only Chosin veteran I have ever met."

"Not that many of us left," Jamieson said with a grin. "Hell, I retired from this place nearly fifteen years ago, after founding it with my partner and building it into a good business. But they called me back when the economy tanked. It seems like old dogs sometimes have forgotten more things than new dogs ever learned."

"So, what have you done for your boss that will convince me that you can do something good for me?" Jamieson continued. "What can you show me?"

McAllister explained how he recently worked on a project for a company that manufactured biological access systems for everything from buildings to secure computers.

"They had one product that required retinal identification, so I came up with 'Keep an Eye Out For Us' on their packages. Then there was another product that used fingerprint and blood vessel identification, so my ad for that one was, 'We're Under Your Thumb!'"

"How did they do?" Jamieson asked.

"As I understand it, they tripled their sales from previous packaging in both cases. Same product, different packaging, different come-ons, big sales boost."

"Can I verify that with your client?"

"Probably," McAllister nodded, adding, however, that it was up to Smythe to release details on his other clients.

"I'll take care of that," Jamieson declared, and McAllister had no doubt that he would be successful.

"So, how long have you been out? And more to the point, how

The Hypocrite

are you handling your return to society?"

McAllister said, "Going on one year," to the first question, adding, "I have some issues sometimes but so far I've been able to keep them under control."

"What kind of issues?" Jamieson asked.

"I try very hard to keep things on an even keel, to keep my temper when someone is being a total ass," McAllister answered. "I don't want to get into a fight with someone if I can avoid it, even though I've been in combat and competed in mixed martial arts while I was on active duty.

"But every so often someone is so out of line that I really have to fight myself mentally to keep from going off. I have to remember what my wife and I have, and what we are working for. I have to remember all that I will lose if I let my temper go.

"Sometimes, if it is really intense I'll just look at the guy and think how his head would look with one of my fifty-caliber rounds making a hole in the front and blowing the living hell out of brain and bone in the back.

"For some reason that gives me a sense of peace and control, and it's easier to just walk away," McAllister concluded.

"Been there, done that," Jamieson said, and then looked beyond McAllister to where Smythe and Anderson were standing just inside the room. They were both silent and had odd looks on their faces, obviously having entered before the conversation between McAllister and Jamieson ended.

"Smythe!" Jamieson called out. "You have the contract. Congratulations!"

He stood up then, and walked around the table close to Smythe. "But I want you to know, it isn't because of your presentation. That was as dull and dry as an old ... well you get the drift. But you have a

The Hypocrite

good man here, with a good mind, and you can thank him for convincing me to go with you.

"Oh," Jamieson continued. "At this business, when one person in a meeting pours himself a cup of coffee or glass of water we offer some to the others. We find it keeps morale on a good level. We expect that of our visitors, too."

Smythe looked as though he was choking on a dead rat, but managed to squeak out an oddly insincere, "Thank you."

They shook hands all around and Jamieson excused himself to go back to work. Anderson led them back to the reception area.

Smythe was coldly quiet as they left the building, walked back to the car and got back inside. He started the engine, left the company parking lot and headed back to I-84 westbound.

Only when he was safely back in the flow of traffic did he speak.

"Should have figured," Smythe said.

"Should have figured what?" McAllister responded.

"Two Marines, alone in a conference room, cooking up some scheme between you."

"The only scheme," McAllister said, "was to convince him that we could do the job. He asked about some of my previous work, I gave him two examples and he was sold. Nothing more, nothing less."

"Yeah, sure. As if I'd believe a couple of jarheads," Smythe retorted.

McAllister turned then, and looking directly at Smythe, said, "You know, Moran, calling a Marine a 'jarhead' when you aren't eligible to be a Marine is the same as using the N-word in a room full of black people when you aren't black."

"I'll call you jarhead, I'll call you anything I want," Smythe yelled, getting back into the mood he was in on the trip to Jamieson's plant earlier that day. But this time McAllister just kept staring at

The Hypocrite

Smythe, his gaze hard, cold and unwavering.

Smythe finally took his eyes off the road and tried to stare back at McAllister, but found himself looking into a pair of eyes that seemed not to be looking at him so much as through him.

Smythe suddenly shivered as a cold chill went up his spine, and he couldn't help but think that McAllister was envisioning his face full of bullet holes and the back of his head spread all over the inside of his Lexus.

Smythe was the first to break the stare between them, using as an excuse the need to keep his eyes on the road.

But for the first time in all their encounters he could feel McAllister's eyes boring into his head for several long minutes more. Eventually, McAllister looked straight ahead and then took in the scenery on the way back to Rocky Hill. It was country at first but then as they neared Vernon, Manchester and East Hartford the population increased, as did the traffic.

The rest of the ride was in total silence, but Smythe couldn't shake the feeling that he was no longer in control and he may well be in way over his head.

Chapter 6

A Taste of Discipline
(The Wife and Dogwood Trees)

Moran Smythe lived ostentatiously.

Despite his claims of anti-materialism his home was a showcase of modern living on the high end of the social scale. There was a lot of glass, often inefficient glass that faced north and east to take advantage of views of the city lights from Hartford, but was virtually useless as an insulator during cold New England winters.

While the office was on the northern side of Rocky Hill, Smythe had never been happy with its elevation just slightly above the flood plain from the Connecticut River. When searching for a home site he found a spot further south but still in Rocky Hill that was nearly 150 feet in elevation. The height gave the house a clear view of the river to the east, with the Silas Deane Highway and I-91 to the west, thus out of sight and not spoiling the view.

His heating bills were high in winter and his electricity bills shot up in the summer as the central air conditioner struggled to deal with the occasional heat wave when the temperatures hit ninety degrees for a week or so. His furnishings were ultra-modern inside and

The Hypocrite

he had every possible amenity outside for gracious living.

When one of the other elders was finally able to buy a new outdoor grill to replace the aging model he had in his yard—a purchase for which the elder saved for nearly two years—Smythe responded by immediately purchasing an even larger stainless steel model with a dozen features he wouldn't and couldn't use. He made a point of letting everyone know he still had the quintessential grill.

When water features became popular Smythe hired stone masons who installed one in his backyard and built a wall with a niche for the grill and a fire feature with stone seats nearby. He had seen a similar layout on television one weekend, and even though it was rarely used, the water feature had to be drained every fall to prevent the lines from freezing. Nonetheless, Smythe owned these extravagences to announce to one and all his arrogant view of his own success.

This arrogance worried the elders, all of whom had been invited to his home for occasional picnics and prayer meetings. The object of these gatherings, at least officially, was fellowship and prayer, but every time there was an event at the Smythe home it turned into an opportunity for Smythe to show off his possessions.

His braggadocio irritated virtually everyone in the church. Their adherence to the teachings of Jesus Christ called for humility, a character trait that seemed unknown to Smythe. It was perfectly acceptable according to the teachings of the Bible to be successful in business and life, in fact it was preferred. But excessive outward manifestations of material success were not looked upon kindly.

Regardless, Smythe was proud of what he had accomplished in life and continually told The Wife how fortunate she was that he had picked her, and that he provided for her. He drove home the point that without him she would be cast out into a cold, cruel world. Un-

The Hypocrite

fortunately for The Wife, she believed him, or at least appeared to believe him.

So, she acknowledged Smythe's claims when he told her that she would have no other options without him, or at the very least she was disinclined to argue, fight back or leave him. But that didn't mean she liked it. She endured it, and in doing so she hardly ever spoke unless authorized by Smythe. Even when the elders and their families visited their home, she minimized her mingling and socializing.

On the Thursday when Smythe and McAllister went to Union for the client pitch at Jamieson's plant, The Wife was at home, cleaning the house, doing a bit of shopping, then preparing dinner, her usual routine. Smythe left the office somewhere between 5 p.m. and 6 p.m. each day and demanded that dinner be ready to eat the instant he entered the house.

It was up to The Wife to know when that would be, even though he never considered giving her a call to tell her he was leaving the office. She developed a system of having part of the dinner ready to eat, so she could put food in front of Smythe the instant he sat down.

The main course would be nearly ready, usually in need of just some reheating or a few minutes of cooking to finish it off. After a few false starts, and some additional trial and error, she developed a workable approach that kept Smythe from blowing up and throwing his food, and kept her from whatever form of punishment he decided should be her due for not having his dinner ready when he was ready.

But that routine changed drastically on the night after the visit to Union. Smythe didn't appear at his usual time—or usual time frame—and The Wife wasn't sure exactly what to do.

Back at Smythe Partners Ltd., Smythe and McAllister went wordlessly to their respective offices after completing the trip. In an

The Hypocrite

effort to regain control and his manliness, Smythe got up from his desk about a half-hour before quitting time and stuck his head into McAllister's office.

"Have you begun working on the Jamieson account?" It was more of a demand than a question.

McAllister actually had gone to work on the new project the second he sat down at his desk. He really enjoyed Jamieson's company, was still somewhat in awe of the man's participation in such an historic battle, and wanted to show the new client what he could do when motivated.

"Typing it up here, boss," McAllister responded, stealing part of a line from the 1960s Paul Newman movie, Cool Hand Luke. He choked back the urge to start humming the melody from the "Plastic Jesus" song from the same movie.

Smythe, however, wasn't a movie buff and had no idea how to respond to that comment. He wasn't sure if McAllister was trying to smooth things over, or making fun of him. He had doubts about McAllister's intent and Moran Smythe was a man who wanted certainties, not doubts.

Instead of hashing it out or just asking McAllister what he meant by that statement, Smythe turned on his heel, stomped down the spiral staircase, and left the building without a word to anyone. He did, however, slam the front door with a resounding BANG that shook the building and resulted in nearly every worker in the back room streaming out to the reception area.

"What's going on? What was the bang? Was it an explosion?" Ken Wilson asked Lemming.

Lemming, seated at her desk with a look that alternated between stunned and clueless, had no explanation and said nothing to the others. Smythe didn't talk to her before leaving, and she had no

The Hypocrite

idea what had transpired that day. There wasn't even any discourse between Smythe and McAllister, at least none that she heard, and she didn't have an inkling what caused Smythe's erratic behavior.

Eventually, everyone returned to their work areas, but by then it was nearly quitting time and they all began shutting down their computers and preparing to leave. Upstairs, McAllister was doing the same thing, and as usual, he copied all of his work from that day to a flash drive.

As usual, instead of putting the flash drive into his desk, McAllister put it into his coat pocket. He had a nagging sense that if he didn't follow this routine every day all his progress from the day's work would disappear.

Smythe, meanwhile, drove in his Lexus toward Wethersfield, quickly arriving at the center. He pulled into a parking space in front of a local eatery and bar, just down the street from the historic seed company buildings in the center of Old Wethersfield.

The bar was dimly lit, served basic bar food, and displayed a simple arrangement of tables along the windowed wall by the street. A few more tables took up the space between the front windows, the bar itself, and a few booths at the far end of the room along the side wall. In the back, a kitchen turned out sandwiches, wraps, grinders, fries, and a small list of salads.

The room could seat about forty people comfortably, and was about half-full, but Smythe ignored the other patrons and made for an empty seat at the end of the mahogany bar. He sat on the swivel stool, noted absent-mindedly that he was glad it had a tall padded back, and put his feet up on the brass rail running the length of the bar about six inches up from the floor.

The bartender quickly appeared in front of him, asking "What can I get you?"

The Hypocrite

Smythe ordered a shot of bar whiskey and a bottle of domestic beer. The bartender pulled the beer from a nearby cooler, and poured the shot without comment. Before the bartender was two steps away Smythe had downed the shot and ordered another. The bartender poured the second one as quickly as the first, but this time Smythe slowed down and sipped alternately at the shot and then the beer.

The cheap whiskey burned the back of his throat before exploding in Smythe's gut, but that was the sensation he was seeking and he was glad to find it at low cost.

Smythe sipped slowly at the second shot and first beer, staring down at his hands or at times at his reflection in the huge mirror behind the bar. The pace around him picked up as the after-work crowd stopped in for a drink or a bite to eat, or both, but Smythe kept to himself, neither looking at nor speaking to anyone else.

When he finished the second shot and first beer he ordered another of each, taking his time with these also. As time slipped away the bartender could hear an occasional mutter from Smythe's direction, and began to watch him warily, but surreptitiously. In Connecticut a bartender is held liable for the actions of drunken customers and the owner of this establishment was especially strict on those who appeared to be near their limit.

Smythe's mutterings grew increasingly hostile.

"Who the hell does that punk think he is? Talk to me that way just because he was in the Marines? He's damn lucky I didn't pull over and kick his ass all over the highway just to make a point.

"My ancestors founded this colony. They were pillars of the community. Without them there wouldn't have been a colony. Who is this upstart? Where did his family originate? How long have they been in this country? One generation, two at best? And he has the temerity to question me and my motives?"

The Hypocrite

As the night wore on Smythe's mood grew malevolent and the muttered threats were verging on lethal. He finished the third shot and the second beer, and after thinking about it ordered one last beer.

It was nearly 8 p.m. now, and although he was clearly upset Smythe had not become loud or abusive. He was keeping to himself and the bartender decided to give him another beer while making a mental note to cut him off if Smythe asked for any more. The bartender had no way of knowing that Smythe's system did not handle alcohol well and burned it off very slowly, which was one reason why Smythe didn't drink very often.

In fact, when he did drink, Smythe had worse hangovers than many other people of his hulking size, and would suffer for most of the next day after drinking only a moderate amount of booze.

Smythe drank the beer quicker than his previous drinks. He placed two twenty-dollar bills on the bar and told the bartender, "Keep the change." The bartender thanked him for the five-dollar tip, and Smythe walked out, steady on his feet, but seething in his heart. He drove home carefully, observing the speed limit, red lights and STOP signs, and soon pulled into his driveway.

Inside, The Wife was dozing on the huge, black leather couch in the living room, but heard the sound of his car door slam and was instantly awake. Fortunately, Smythe took about five steps toward the front door when he remembered that he had left his briefcase in the car.

As he retraced his steps, The Wife hurried out to the kitchen, nuking his dinner in the microwave. Outside, Smythe dropped his briefcase as the liquor caught up with his reactions. It hit the ground, opened and his papers scattered, causing another delay in his entrance as he retrieved them.

By the time he entered the house he was back in a foul mood

The Hypocrite

and barely nodded to The Wife asking only, "Is dinner ready?"

His tone carried the implied threat that it had better be ready, and The Wife was relieved when she answered, "It's on the table for you."

He headed to the kitchen without speaking. She followed at a discreet pace and stood quietly off to the side as he dug in, consuming the meal quickly, but without comment.

"I'll be expecting you to take care of matters in the bedroom tonight," he told her with a direct stare that indicated he expected no contradictions. He then ordered her to get him a bottle of beer from the fridge, a true departure from his normal activities.

The Wife nodded silently, brought the beer, and immediately left the kitchen, stopping first at the upstairs bathroom where she freshened herself. She then walked straight to the expansive master bedroom with its wall of windows overlooking the winding Connecticut River. The room was decorated with tens of thousands of dollars of furniture and art, including a huge king-sized bed that once caused an elder—with a well-known sense of humor—to question if Smythe had issues.

She turned off the light, a habit ingrained long ago, slipped under the covers and waited.

The Wife wasn't sure how much time elapsed before Smythe entered the room. She dozed off, but then heard the click of the old-fashioned—Smythe called it 'antique'—door latch, and then the sounds of Smythe undressing.

She steeled herself for what she knew was headed her way, and after a minute felt his bulk sink in on his side of the bed, and in a few seconds the foul odor of whiskey, beer and bad breath directly in her face.

Smythe never engaged in foreplay—useless preliminaries, he

The Hypocrite

called them—and told her often that it was not the man's duty to satisfy or even please his wife, but it was her duty to please and satisfy him! He was never kind or gentle, and his sexual advances could at best be described as painful, although brutal or violent were also accurate descriptions.

But The Wife didn't know that because she long ago learned to send her mind to a different, far better place, a place where there was beauty, the perfume of flowers, the hum of bees, the gentle babbling of a cool brook. She too was raised a Christian, and in the worst times she thought of the suffering of Jesus as he was betrayed by some of his followers and then brutalized by the Roman soldiers, leading to his crucifixion.

Tonight she was thinking of dogwoods, the trees that grew in this section of the country and bloomed at Easter time each year. She concentrated on remembering how the leaves were adopted by Christians as symbols of the crucifixion and ultimately the Resurrection. She remembered the legend that said the four petals of the dogwood flowers form a cross, and they have marks on their outer edge which many believe symbolize nail marks.

The Wife remembered that the center of the flower resembles a crown like the crown of thorns that Jesus was forced to wear, and that the red berries represent his blood. She continued to concentrate on the dogwood and neither felt nor heard her husband as he used her body as though it were just another of his possessions.

Tonight, Smythe was drunk and abusive, but the only real departure from the norm was his drunkenness. Usually, Smythe didn't drink, but he was just as abusive when sober.

Over and over she recited the litany of the dogwood, its history and its parts. She could nearly smell the blossoms and hear the humming of insects and honey bees.

The Hypocrite

She didn't know when he got off her. She was concentrating on the droning of the bees and somewhere along the way realized that she actually was hearing Smythe's snoring, not bees. She gingerly left the bed, feeling pain in her midsection, and made her way to the bathroom.

Once there she gave herself a visual inspection, noticing that she had bled, not an unusual result of his assaults on her body, but the blood was dried and she didn't appear to be bleeding further. The Wife stepped into the shower, turned the water on hot and hard, and stood for a very, very long time, just letting the stream hit her body in a futile attempt to wash away a feeling that could never be erased by soap and water.

She finally reached to the faucet controls, turned off the shower, stepped outside the stall and dried herself with a huge terrycloth towel. She kept a spare set of nightclothes in the bathroom closet and taking the pajamas closest to her, she dressed, then returned to the living room with a quilt, once again sleeping on the couch.

The Wife awoke in the morning to the sounds of Smythe in the bathroom and hurried out to the kitchen to put on the coffee. When he entered the room about twenty minutes later she asked him politely, "Will you be eating breakfast here this morning?"

Smythe nodded his assent then told her, "Two eggs over, and I don't want the whites runny. Toast too."

"Jam or butter?" was her only response.

"Both."

The Wife quickly and efficiently made the breakfast, setting the plate before him in less than ten minutes.

"Will there be anything else?" she asked.

"Yes," he answered with a level of force that did not sound positive. "I know that you don't have much in the way of passion, but you

The Hypocrite

could at least pretend that you are enjoying our marriage bed. I don't ask much from you. I provide you with everything you have, which you would not have without me, and a little appreciation for my efforts doesn't seem like too much to ask."

The Wife stood with her eyes downcast, and murmured, "I'll try to do better. I'll do my best to please you." She could have been standing in front of a nobleman in the European Middle Ages. The moment only lacked a "Yes, M'Lord" response.

Smythe didn't respond, and in a few more minutes stood up, left the room and headed out for the office. He didn't say goodbye and he gave her absolutely no sign of affection.

The Wife watched his car leave the driveway and head for the Silas Deane. She stood looking down the street for a long ten minutes, fearing that he might have forgotten something and would return unexpectedly. It wasn't that far to the office and if he was so inclined Smythe could be back to the house in a matter of just a few minutes.

After she was sure he was gone, The Wife went to the kitchen and reached far back in the cupboard where she kept baking supplies, pulling out a small tin of fine tea. She brewed a pot, got a small, delicate, exquisite tea cup and saucer from her china closet, and poured herself a cup, adding milk but no sugar.

The Wife tried so hard, so very hard to put the previous night behind her and take a small bit of pleasure from the simple act of sipping a cup of tea. But Smythe's assaults had been going on for too long and her resistance to his brutality was too low.

Suddenly she began shaking uncontrollably, and the spasms were followed almost immediately by a flood of tears. They were huge globules of salt water, accompanied by intense, wracking sobs that barely touched upon the depth of her pain and unhappiness. The

The Hypocrite

sobs and tears continued unabated for nearly an hour and it seemed that she would die from sadness.

She couldn't help but think of all the promise that their marriage held originally. They met when Smythe applied for a job at her father's business, located in the same building that now housed Smythe Partners. Smythe was a smooth talker and charmed both The Wife and her father.

Although The Wife was considered to be on a par with her father in the business operations, Smythe soon was named a partner. Not long after his promotion, Smythe asked her father for his daughter's hand in marriage, a somewhat old-fashioned approach that nonetheless made Smythe's stature swell in his future father-in-law's eyes.

They had a traditional church wedding and she was resplendent in her white gown, looking forward to a future that held nothing but promise. But only a few months after their wedding, tragedy struck.

A hit-and-run driver ran a STOP sign late at night as her father was returning from a meeting of a local business organization, hitting the driver's side of his car, striking him directly and killing him instantly. The other car fled and there were no witnesses.

Within a week of the funeral, The Wife discovered to her total amazement, that although her father left her most of his sizeable financial holdings, he left the business to Smythe! In less than a week it became Smythe Partner's Ltd., and although The Wife had an important position in her father's firm, Smythe put his mark on the new version of the business by demoting her and essentially relegating her to a non-essential status.

The initial promise of their union dissipated literally overnight, and looking back The Wife was broken hearted. But despite her somewhat frail appearance, internally she was strong and finally the

The Hypocrite

shaking abated, and she brought her sobs under control.

Smythe sometimes came home in mid-morning and it wouldn't do for him to find her in such a state and looking the way she did. That would make Smythe very unhappy. Everyone who knew him, knew that making Moran Smythe unhappy could have only one result—and it wouldn't be pretty.

Chapter 7

Riding the Almighty

If anything unusual occurred at Smythe Partners Ltd., on the day of the client visit to Jack Jamieson's business in Union, it didn't show the following day when McAllister arrived at work.

He entered the front door as usual, finding that Lemming was not at her desk, as usual. He ascended the spiral staircase to his office, noting that the door to Smythe's office was closed tight, which also was not unusual.

The only question McAllister had was whether Smythe was in the office or had not yet arrived. McAllister learned early on that the presence of Smythe's car in its reserved space did not mean Smythe was in the building. Similarly, there were times when the car was not in its space, but Smythe was inside. There probably were good reasons for the seeming disparities, but McAllister didn't care enough to figure it out.

He went into his office, switched the computer on, and took the flash drive containing the previous day's work from his coat pocket. When the computer finished booting up, he inserted the drive into the appropriate slot and then walked back downstairs to the confer-

The Hypocrite

ence room to see if anyone had made coffee. He was in luck, finding a nearly full pot on the warmer. He poured a cup, added some cream from the fridge, and walked back up to his office, still not encountering a soul.

McAllister heard some murmured conversation from the area of the marketing office while he was pouring his coffee, but decided against going back for a chit chat. He knew that today was not a day for discussions around the water cooler or coffee pot or anywhere else. If he wanted things to stay calm and quiet, it was a day to work with no breaks.

He again ascended the staircase and reentered his office, sitting down at the desk, taking a sip of coffee and then calling up his client files. And that is when the usual turned unusual.

They weren't there. As in, they were nowhere to be found in the company data base. There simply were no files that had originated in his user directory or in any other directory. McAllister did a search of the entire system but it came back as "no file found."

Fortunately, when he clicked on the icon for the "D" drive, he found the information on his flash drive just as he intended, so the issue was theft, not a virus. But that flash drive contained only a few days worth of work. That in itself was not a long-term problem because he also was in the habit of making backups of the flash drives he made in the office, one for the office and one that he took home.

McAllister talked often with Julia about the strange goings on at Smythe's and months ago they agreed over coffee at the kitchen table that, to adequately protect himself, he should backup the backups. He kept a supply of flash drives in his desk drawer containing all of his work going back to the first day, and those in turn were backed up by copies he took home. McAllister also locked his desk at night, but that was only a temporary barrier as both Smythe and Lemming had

The Hypocrite

master keys to all the desks and file cabinets in the office.

McAllister opened the top drawer on the left side of the desk and reached inside for the box of backup flash drives, but just as he discovered when he went searching for the files in the computer, the box was not there.

Bruce McAllister could never be described as a neatnik. Even though he was always squared away and ready for inspections in the Marines, once he got back home McAllister was pretty much the opposite. That was the one facet of his personality that could get to Julia on occasion, although she long ago decided that, if that was the worst thing she encountered in their marriage, then life really wasn't too bad.

He could be faulted for having a messy desk or deciding that the terms "laundry hamper" and "floor" were interchangeable especially regarding the final disposition of his dirty gym clothes. But the one thing about his storage system—or lack of it—was that McAllister knew where he put things, where he left things, and where they were in the general scheme.

If Julia straightened up his desk in his home office, it was virtually certain that he would know that something was moved, and not just because the piles were neater or that a dust cloth had obviously made its presence known in his work area. McAllister invariably would need a document, know precisely where on his desk it should be, at least within a few layers of documents going top to bottom. If the document appeared somewhere else, he knew it had been moved and not by him.

Thus, even though McAllister's desk drawer at Smythe Partners tended to appear as a recently vacated battlefield, he still knew that someone went through it, simply because things were not in the general area where he had left them. But most importantly, his box of backup flash drives was no longer there.

The Hypocrite

He quickly opened the center drawer, which also showed evidence of tampering, as well as the two large drawers on the right side of the desk. Everything was a mess in all of the drawers—not his mess, but the mess left by someone rummaging through them—and none of them contained his box of backup flash drives. Whoever had been in his office, and McAllister knew exactly who that was, had not just tampered with the computer files and ransacked his desk drawers, she had stolen his flash drives too.

McAllister initially considered storming downstairs and confronting Lemming directly, but he knew from experience that he would lose if he employed that tactic. Predictably, she would complain to Smythe, saying McAllister was harassing her. Smythe would take her side, and she would get off without so much as a warning, while McAllister would have to worry about his future employment at Smythe Partners, Ltd.

So, he sat back and thought. First and foremost, he wasn't really in a bind as far as today's work was concerned since he had the second flash drive. He called up the file he was working on the previous day, and displayed what he had accomplished so far on his screen, just in case Smythe decided to play cat and mouse today.

But as much as he was inclined to turn out the copy for Jamieson's products as quickly as possible, he found himself completely engrossed in the situation at hand. Today, he knew, was not going to be a very productive day.

For more than an hour, McAllister kept going over his options, seeking out new ones, looking for the flaws in his reasoning. But no matter what he considered, the ultimate result of every possible option was that it would have no impact other than cause trouble for himself, given the weird relationship between Smythe and Lemming.

Around 11 a.m., McAllister again went downstairs for coffee.

The Hypocrite

This time Lemming was sitting at her desk, doing nothing, hands folded, attempting to look angelic, which didn't work.

There was fresh coffee again, and McAllister reminded himself to thank whoever in the back offices made it. Generally speaking, both in the Marines and in corporate America, it was the duty of the person who took the last cup to make a fresh pot. McAllister could make good coffee and never minded when his turn arose, but that didn't happen very often.

He generally didn't drink more than two cups each day, and never after lunch since the caffeine would start working on him in the middle of the night and sleep would be difficult. He fixed a second cup just like the first one, and again headed for his office.

"Seen Moran today?" he asked Lemming.

"He's in his office. You should know that," she snapped.

"The door has been closed all morning and I haven't even heard him talking. So how would I know where he is? What's he up to, anyway?" McAllister knew there would be a wise reply of some sort to that question and he didn't even stop walking toward the stairs.

"If he wanted you to know what he is doing I'm sure he would have told you," he heard Lemming say as he ascended. McAllister never broke stride, didn't look back and didn't answer. She smirked to herself, completely misreading his response.

Lemming had indeed sabotaged McAllister's work the previous night. She didn't know why Smythe was so upset when he left the office but she correctly deduced that it had something to do with McAllister. As soon as he got in his truck and headed out the driveway, she went up to his office and began systematically deleting files. It was Lemming's way to show her disdain for McAllister and her loyalty to Smythe. She could have simply accessed his computer from her desk downstairs, but Lemming was angry, hence her trek up to his

The Hypocrite

office where she went on a rampage of destruction. In her pea brain, she didn't just want to annoy McAllister, she wanted to make him feel violated.

Lemming didn't know about the backup flash drives because going up the stairs was a major effort for her. But when she saw the box in McAllister's drawer she had a good idea what it contained and took one at random to display on the screen.

When her suspicions had been confirmed, she took the entire box out of the drawer, ejected the one flash drive from the computer, and threw them all in the downstairs garbage can. Later that night the janitorial service emptied it into the dumpster outside. McAllister actually could have retrieved his flash drives if he didn't mind a little "dumpster diving" but he didn't know what Lemming had done or how to rectify it, other than making copies of files on the flash drives in his office at home.

He figured that Lemming was enjoying her little charade but McAllister really didn't care about her. Instead, he entered his office, sat at his desk, reviewed his work, decided to make some additions to it, and sipped his coffee in between keystrokes. He became so engrossed in the project for Jamieson that it was lunchtime before he knew it.

At the stroke of noon, McAllister saved all his work, both to the new computer file he created and to his flash drive. He took the flash drive as a precaution and left his office for lunch.

Lemming was still at her desk and suddenly took an interest in McAllister's activities.

"Going out for lunch today?" she asked, with a tone that implied the unpleasantness of the morning was suddenly gone.

"That would appear to be the case," he responded, giving Lemming a taste of her own medicine.

The Hypocrite

He continued out to the parking lot and started his truck. It was mid-autumn now, he had well over six months of work at Smythe Partners behind him, but he still didn't feel as though he was a permanent part of the corporate landscape. The exchange with Lemming served as an exclamation point to that feeling.

Initially, he figured it was time for a trip to the center of Old Wethersfield and a sandwich from the deli there. But, in one of those strange quirks of fate that happen from time to time, McAllister changed his mind and instead headed for a nearby fast food restaurant with a drive-through window.

He ordered a small version of their signature burger and two cartons of low fat milk. The line moved quickly and he was in and out in less than two minutes.

Along with deciding not to go to Wethersfield, McAllister also decided he would bring his lunch back to his office. In truth, he was feeling guilty about not working enough on Jamieson's project that morning, and he figured he could make up some time if he ate at his desk and worked through lunch.

He pulled into the parking lot, grabbing a spot that was the farthest from the entrance to the building, but under a tree. The leaves were turning bright yellow and they still would keep the afternoon sun off of his truck, which in turn would keep it cool for him at the end of the day.

The truck door usually swung closed on its own, since he kept the vehicle well lubricated, but there was a slight downhill slant to the parking lot in this area, and with his hands filled with his lunch, he was forced to close the door by pushing it with his back. It closed with a soft "click" and he walked to the entrance.

He also had to juggle his lunch while he opened the door to the office, and—remembering Smythe slamming it the previous evening,

The Hypocrite

scaring the daylights out of everyone in the building—McAllister closed it quietly so as to not disturb anyone else.

He thought about that later, how so many seemingly disconnected and relatively innocent occurrences came together one right after the other. Lemming was not at her desk and McAllister figured that she too went out to lunch.

But, as he approached the stairs, McAllister suddenly thought about Smythe, and how he was in his office all morning, not appearing at any time to check on the business, not even talking on the phone. McAllister had no way of knowing that Smythe had consumed way more than his limit the night before and was suffering from a brutal hangover.

If McAllister did know, he would have laughed. He tried to be a good person but he never classified himself or thought of himself as a saint. If he knew that Smythe was actually sleeping off the excess booze from the night before, his primary reaction probably would have been "serves him right."

Nonetheless, he did have a sliver of mercy in his soul and he decided that whatever was going on, Smythe obviously wanted quiet and his privacy. McAllister ascended the stairs quietly, making virtually no noise whatsoever.

In the next minute, he wished to God that he had slammed doors and stomped around like a madman. He reached the top of the stairs and noticed that either Smythe had left the office or someone had gone inside, because the door was open—not wide, but several inches.

Then McAllister saw Smythe and what he saw nearly made him throw up, even though he had been exposed to some pretty gruesome sights in the war. Smythe was in his seat at his desk, but the chair was swiveled out to the side. His head was back on the chair, as though he

The Hypocrite

was sleeping.

But his trousers were down around his heels along with his underwear, and in between his widely spread thighs was none other than Gail Lemming. She too was partly undressed. Her giant-sized panties were on the floor, her dress was pulled up nearly to her shoulders and great globules of fat hung off her like Spanish moss on a southern oak.

She and Smythe were engaged in a sexual act, and their positions made virtually all of her private parts visible, in addition to a considerable amount of Smythe's anatomy.

It was not a pleasant sight. It was not a pretty sight. It was not the kind of sight that anyone in their right mind would want to see by accident or on purpose, because it would be indelibly etched into their memory no matter how hard they tried to erase it. But there it was, right in McAllister's direct line of view.

He looked into their faces and realized they both had their eyes closed—lost in the throes of ecstasy as he later explained it to Julia. Or, in Smythe's case, perhaps that he simply could not bear to watch what he was doing with Lemming.

In less than a heartbeat, McAllister did a noiseless about face and went down the staircase as quietly as he had ascended it a minute earlier. But he was angry! Here was evidence as to why Smythe gave preference to Lemming whenever an issue arose in the office. But once again, the answer to one question merely raised another question—Why? Why Lemming? Smythe might be an assbite but he had a pretty wife, and if that wasn't working out for him he appeared to have enough money to buy someone, anyone for that matter, who would be light years better than Lemming.

McAllister thought for a minute and then a devious plan erupted in his mind. He turned toward the door to the parking lot, opened it quietly, stepped outside and then slammed it with all the effort that

The Hypocrite

Smythe put into doing the same thing the night before.

As the office behind him erupted McAllister strolled over to his truck, opened the door and made a show of looking in the back section for something, in case one of his co-workers exited the office. While McAllister was covering his tracks outside, all hell was breaking loose inside.

When McAllister slammed the door, Lemming and Smythe quickly disengaged upstairs, while the staff in the back offices came boiling out into the reception area downstairs—led by Ken Wilson—just as they had done the night before. They milled around for several minutes totally in the dark as to what had caused the noise.

Back upstairs, Smythe and Lemming got dressed as quickly as possible, which caused considerable thumping and bumping on the floor that could be heard downstairs, further causing a series of knowing looks between the staff, but gave no clue as to the source of the bang.

To make matters worse, Smythe's haste and his partially undressed state combined to make his efforts to get dressed beyond difficult. His trousers were pulled up only halfway when he tripped, smacking his chin on the corner of his desk. Then, to literally add injury to insult, as he attempted to right himself, Smythe's knee smacked the hard, pointed corner of his desk, the sharp edge driving straight into the soft tissue on the side of his kneecap. The pain was excruciating and would stay with him for weeks.

Figuring it wouldn't be in anyone's best interests to stay in the reception area, Wilson started moving the other workers back to their offices. Try as he might he couldn't reverse the situation fast enough and most of the staff were still in the front, when Lemming, looking as though she just emerged from a wind tunnel, came down the spiral staircase at an atypically fast pace.

The Hypocrite

Wilson was standing next to the door and Lemming fixed him with a malevolent glare. "What did you do?" she screamed at Wilson. "What did you do?"

"What the hell are you talking about, Lemming?" Wilson yelled back. He suddenly didn't care what happened from this point on. He was fed up to the gills with Smythe, Lemming and anything that had anything to do with them. "We heard a noise out here again, sounded like an explosion and we came out to see if everything is okay."

"That was the door slamming, and you know it," Lemming hissed.

Wilson stormed out of the office, needing some time and space, and saw McAllister climbing out of his truck cab at the far end of the parking lot. McAllister appeared to be just arriving, but he actually was retrieving his cell phone, which had fallen to the floor on the passenger's side, and which McAllister discovered only after he had left the building a few minutes earlier.

"Did you hear a loud noise?" Wilson called over to McAllister. "Like an explosion?" he added.

"Yeah, I think it was a sonic boom!" McAllister replied. "I saw something in the paper about the Air National Guard doing some joint exercises up at Bradley Airport this week. They must have some military jets in the area."

Wilson headed back into the building.

"I need to turn the phones back on," Lemming was saying. "Everyone get away from my desk."

By now Smythe was standing at the base of the spiral staircase, wearing a look that was half angry, half perplexed and unsuccessfully attempting to hide the damage to his chin.

"What was that loud noise?" he demanded to no one in particular.

The Hypocrite

"I think it was a sonic boom," Wilson replied as everyone else remained silent.

"Thonic boom?" Smythe asked, the injury to his mouth already affecting his speech. His look changed instantly from perplexed to incredulous.

"Yeah, the Air National Guard is supposed to be doing some kind of joint exercises at Bradley this week. I think it was them," Wilson added. He omitted that he had just learned that information from McAllister.

Smythe gave him a look of disbelief, muttering, "Thonic Boom, my atth," under his breath and turned back upstairs limping noticeably as he ascended. Wilson shook his head in disgust and walked back to his office.

Thirty seconds later, McAllister reentered the office, finding only Lemming and two graphics artists who stayed in the front long enough to get themselves some coffee.

"Hi, guys. What's up?" McAllister asked cheerily.

"There was a sonic boom," Lemming growled. "Didn't you hear it?"

"Sonic boom?" McAllister asked, feigning his own version of incredulity. "I didn't hear a sonic boom. I haven't heard a sonic boom in years."

With that he turned to the stairs and headed back to his office, a slight smile tugging at the corners of his mouth.

McAllister went back to work, but really didn't work. Smythe's office door remained closed all afternoon, and while he didn't know what happened while he was outside, he could only surmise that it must have been quite a show.

He tried to work, but McAllister couldn't help replaying the disgusting scene in Smythe's office and imagining the response to the slamming of the front door. So he counted. Sixty seconds per minute,

The Hypocrite

sixty minutes per hour, four hours until he could escape The Zoo.

Ultimately, 14,400 seconds went by and McAllister packed up. He made another copy on his flash drive, put it in his pocket, sent his work to Smythe by email just for the hell of it, and locked his desk drawers. He was certain Lemming had a master key but it wasn't likely that she would carry it with her. If she had to go up and down the stairs twice in the same hour, well, tough luck for her.

Finally, McAllister was in his truck, on the road, and blessedly, back in his own driveway.

He walked inside, took Julia by the arm, walked out to the kitchen table, sat her down, sat down across from her and in excruciating detail told her everything that had happened at Smythe Partners that day.

When he was finished, she was silent for a long minute.

Then Julia reached both of her hands across the table and grasped both of his. She looked deep into his eyes, and with tears brimming in hers, finally said, in her softest, kindest most loving voice, "Hon. Can I have some of your scotch? The good stuff?"

Chapter 8

Government Interference

The luncheon that McAllister was supposed to attend in July seemed as though it occurred ages ago, instead of just a few months, but in November the issues that concerned the elders of The Church of the Lord still were on the front burner.

Their congregation was growing steadily and while they still held their services and meetings at a rented hall, most congregants agreed that it was time to build their own church. After a year of searching, false starts and negotiations that went nowhere, the elders discovered and put a deposit on a parcel of land with a view of the river, near Dividend Pond.

Although there were many benefits to the parcel, including access roads and the river view, there also were a number of drawbacks. The parcel was located near a small, mostly developed industrial park, and churches were a permitted use in that zone. But, many of the nearby buildings were constructed before modern zoning and environmental regulations went into effect, and their owners benefitted from being "grandfathered."

The Hypocrite

New construction for the church would require a host of governmental approvals. The building issues were seen as manageable since the congregation included several members who worked in the construction trades. However, the overriding issue blocking the beginning of construction was the application of local, state and federal wetlands regulations.

The topography in that section of Rocky Hill is varied, ranging from the Connecticut River flood plain to steep hills, the tops of which wouldn't see water that high unless the Almighty decides to destroy the world by flood again, which the Bible says he won't. It was on one of these knolls that the elders were planning to build their church.

In accordance with the elders' beliefs and lifestyles, it would not be an opulent edifice. But, it would face both the river and the sunrise in the east, and the plans called for a display of stained glass on that side of the building for the congregation's enjoyment on the Sabbath.

Otherwise the building would be unremarkable. The design called for rooms suitable for worship, Bible classes, and the various forms of outreach embraced by the congregation, including a soup kitchen. The parishioners regularly volunteered for soup kitchen duty at area shelters, especially during cold weather conditions and the holidays. But, they wanted to be more consistent in their efforts and work with the needy population closer to home.

Thus, the building regulations required commercial-sized rest rooms, a commercial kitchen, a plan for garbage disposal, and room to set up tables in addition to the more traditional worship activities. In most respects the building plans appeared to meet all requirements, and the building lot appeared to be perfect for their church. It was perfect, that is, except for that one issue with the topography.

Since the parcel was surrounded by Connecticut River flood

The Hypocrite

plain, issues regarding proximity to water and wetlands were regulated by the US Army Corps of Engineers and the federal Environmental Protection Agency, in addition to state and local regulations.

In fact, so as to be conversant with the issues facing them, each elder and each member of the building committee had a copy of the relevant information: *The Corps of Engineers regulates work and structures that are located in, under or over navigable waters of the United States under Section 10 of the Rivers and Harbors Act of 1899; the discharge of dredged or fill material into waters of the United States under Section 404 of the Clean Water Act; and the transportation of dredged material for the purpose of disposal in the ocean (regulated by the Corps under Section 103 of the Marine Protection, Research and Sanctuaries Act). "Waters of the United States" are navigable waters, tributaries to navigable waters, wetlands adjacent to those waters and/or isolated wetlands that have a demonstrated interstate commerce connection.*

In theory, that should have posed no problems for the proposed project, other than to insure that it met all applicable regulations, and that the Corps signed off on it for the local wetlands authority. But times were hard, the size of government at all levels was under constant fire, and bureaucrats found themselves scrambling to ensure that all applications from the simplest to the most complicated were given the same level of scrutiny.

To the members of The Church of the Lord that increased scrutiny suddenly became a major stumbling block to fulfilling their dream of building a church. What should have been perfunctory reviews and approval of the building plans turned into a maze of bureaucratic obfuscation and delays that left the elders baffled and frustrated.

But a ray of hope shined through earlier in the year, when Moran Smythe declared that, with his knowledge of government regula-

The Hypocrite

tions and his contacts on the state and federal levels, he would be able to resolve the issue in the church's favor. The issue, as it turned out, was that a bureaucrat on the federal level interpreted the regulations regarding distance from regulated wetlands in a manner that was unusual, if not outright unique, and his state counterpart decided not to challenge the federal ruling.

The interpretation, as applied by the federal Department of Environmental Protection—and glossed over by reviewers at the Corps of Engineers—was that the proposed building would be too close to a nearby wetland. But, the determination used questionable measurements that were subject to appeal. The parcel had wetlands on two sides, but it also was more than 100 feet above sea level.

On the west side the slope was extraordinarily steep, and while any building would be well outside the boundaries where construction was prohibited based on the vertical climb, it unfortunately was still within those boundaries when measured horizontally. That—according to Smythe at least—was the crux of the issue. It was virtually unheard of to measure distance from a wetland by a horizontal measurement when the building lot was so high above sea level and the wetland. Until now.

The luncheon meeting that caused McAllister such a headache was intended to determine the best approach for dealing with the regulatory agencies and to review the options available to the church. In the end, Moran Smythe convinced the rest of the elders that with an appropriate infusion of cash, in this case $35,000, he could hire an attorney with knowledge and experience in zoning matters on the local, state and federal levels.

Not everyone who sat in on the luncheon was enthused about that concept, especially with the amount set by Smythe. In fact, virtually everyone at lunch that day was shocked by the number Smythe

The Hypocrite

put forward, but no one came prepared with a current knowledge of legal fees and costs associated with that kind of work.

Oddly enough, it was Smythe who was insistent on having McAllister at the luncheon, because even though he didn't like McAllister, Smythe knew him to be creative, with an uncanny ability to think fast on his feet. Smythe figured McAllister would be able to present some scenarios that the others hadn't considered. While appearing to be earnestly seeking McAllister's input, Smythe actually planned that all other scenarios ultimately could be shot down, giving Smythe even more credence when he made his pitch.

McAllister's absence meant that there were fewer options offered to the elders, and a quicker move to the central point—that Smythe should be given money to rectify the situation, through both legal means and personal contacts. In the end, Smythe was forced to play his hand much earlier than he wanted, but he was given the money, albeit grudgingly.

Now it was mid-November and the issue was still unresolved. Construction would have to wait until spring as the ground already was freezing up, and pouring cement for the foundation would be impossible until warmer weather returned. But by spring, when the weather favored renewed construction, there still were permits and approvals that must be secured.

Smythe regularly reported to the elders, that the attorney he hired was "making progress" in his negotiations with the state and federal authorities, but that there were still some "sticking points" that needed to be resolved. Ultimately, Elder Derrick Simpson called the local wetlands agent and asked that the church be given time at the next agency meeting to hash out the problems and determine what needed to be done to resolve them.

Simpson, as the senior elder in the church, usually commu-

The Hypocrite

nicated his intents and actions to the other elders to give them an opportunity for input before action was taken. In this case, he did inform most of the elders, but not Smythe, until the meeting agenda was set.

When Smythe finally found out about the coming meeting—he was tipped off by a church member with a reputation for playing both sides—he hit the roof. He fumed, fussed and stormed back and forth in his office, but he kept it inside his office.

McAllister was aware that something was going on, since it was impossible to miss the noise coming from Smythe's office, but even that was done behind a closed door and the reason behind the outbursts was not clear. However, as happened with some regularity since McAllister went to work for Smythe, a couple of events combined to bring him up to speed on the issue and the impact it could have on his future.

After seeing Lemming and Smythe together in Smythe's office McAllister was beyond disgust and teetering on the verge of quitting, a move that he decided against only because he needed the job and finding another one was not guaranteed. McAllister could only hope that he would not encounter a similar situation in the future, but on Wednesday of the following week, he discovered that there were even more surprises in store for him.

The first thing he saw upon entering the building was that Lemming was wearing an expensive pair of earrings. They were gold with diamond stones set in them, which Lemming confirmed nearly the second he stepped inside the reception area.

"Do you like my diamond earrings?" she inquired. Before McAllister could respond she added, "They were a gift from a close friend." Then she giggled, like a little girl with a big secret.

McAllister said nothing and walked to the staircase, but noticed

The Hypocrite

as he turned away from her that Lemming also was flashing a delicate gold wrist watch, one that he had never seen before. It, too, looked very expensive and he couldn't help but wonder how she could afford such expensive jewelry on what certainly was a yeoman's salary.

Then, almost immediately, he wondered if the jewelry had something to do with Lemming's "off the books" work for Smythe.

McAllister continued on into his office and immediately set to work on the Jamieson account. Smythe came up the stairs about an hour later and stuck his head inside McAllister's office.

"Is that the Jamieson account you're working on?"

When McAllister replied in the affirmative, Smythe ordered him, "Ship what you have done over to me at the end of the day." With that he turned on his heel and left the office.

McAllister was happy to see him go and went back to work on the possible scenarios for Jamieson's packaging. Before he knew it, noon arrived and he prepared to leave for lunch, saving his work to a flash drive and taking it with him. After all he had experienced in the past couple of months, not to mention the last week, McAllister was taking no chances, not in the morning, or at noon, or at night.

He left the building without seeing Lemming again, and drove to Old Wethersfield. Julia had packed him a lunch that morning and he headed straight for the Center Cemetery without stopping at the deli. He parked in his usual spot under the oak tree, which by now was nearly devoid of leaves, turned off the engine and turned on the tunes.

Lunch today was a turkey sandwich, with a small bag of chips, an apple and diet cola—caffeine free. It was good, and although he rarely drank soda of any kind McAllister enjoyed the carbonation of his drink as well as the sandwich Julia had made for him. In addition to the turkey and mayo, it was layered with provolone cheese, thin

The Hypocrite

slices of onion and topped with a huge slice of tomato, just the way he liked it.

McAllister was about halfway through his lunch, enjoying the oldies on the truck radio, and once again staring aimlessly at the entrance to the cemetery, when he had a déjà vu moment. There again was a figure, walking from the entrance toward his truck.

Once again McAllister saw a tall, lean man, and once again, as the figure neared him McAllister recognized Derrick Simpson walking straight toward him. Unlike their chance meeting in July, when Simpson was stern-looking and appeared to be under considerable stress, this time he was smiling as he approached the truck.

"I prayed that you'd be here today," Simpson said with a lop-sided grin.

"Well, Elder, the Good Lord is smiling down on you," McAllister joked back. "Your prayers have been answered. So what's on your mind?"

"Why don't you finish your lunch first, while I go visit my wife's grave? I didn't mean to interrupt your meal. I only need a few minutes, but it's important to me to make sure that my wife knows I haven't forgotten her."

McAllister nodded in agreement and Simpson headed toward his wife's gravestone. He disappeared from McAllister's direct line of sight in a matter of minutes, and McAllister returned to his meal.

When he finished the last bite of the sandwich and wiped away the crumbs of the chips, McAllister took a final drink of his soda, cleaned up the debris, and put it into the brown bag that contained his meal. He then put that in a larger bag he kept in the back so the truck wouldn't become a self-contained garbage wagon. As he finished, he looked up to see Simpson returning.

"We have a problem at the church," Simpson said as soon as

The Hypocrite

he was near enough to speak in a normal tone. "And it involves your boss."

Without waiting for McAllister to respond, Simpson gave a lengthy rundown of the previous year's efforts to gain approval for a new church building and the difficulties encountered in the process. He related why the luncheon meeting in July was so important, although he added that the elders really didn't understand why Smythe was so insistent that McAllister attend, or why he was so angry when McAllister kept his appointment at the bank instead.

Then he got into the meat of the situation—that Smythe had been given $35,000 to pay for legal assistance and possible professional expertise in related matters. But, he recounted that no one had yet met the lawyer who Smythe said was working on their case, or even knew his name! And people were questioning the disposition of the money.

"It's bad enough that Smythe is our treasurer and was given unprecedented authority to spend a large portion of the church savings," Simpson said. "But he also has access to a total of $100,000 and lately he has been ducking our questions about his expenditures.

"So, I took matters into my own hands," Simpson concluded. "I called the local authorities and asked if we could meet to iron out our problems. The man at town hall didn't seem to think we even had a problem and said he hasn't been contacted by anyone but me, especially a lawyer.

"Moran was really mad when I told him we were on the agenda for this week's zoning meeting," Simpson added. "He didn't say much when I told him, but you could see in his eyes that he was one unhappy individual."

"Well, that certainly explains a few things," McAllister finally responded when he could get a word into the conversation.

The Hypocrite

"What things?" Simpson asked.

"He's stomping around his office, snorting and complaining," McAllister revealed. "I can't make out what he's so mad at, because his door is closed. But, you sure can tell that he is not pleased."

Simpson said nothing for a few seconds, digesting what McAllister told him, and suddenly McAllister burst out in laughter.

"What's so funny about all this?" Simpson asked, with a sense of irritation.

"He reminds me of a guy my father used to work with," McAllister said. "Dad used to say the guy had 'hoof-and-mouth disease!'"

"You mean anthrax?" Simpson asked with a look of incredulity.

That prompted another outburst of laughter from McAllister who finally answered, "No. Not anthrax. Dad said the guy was always 'hoofing around, running off at the mouth!'"

McAllister's response hit Simpson's funny bone dead on and he too started to laugh. He finally told McAllister, "Oh, that's him. That's Smythe right down to his shoelaces."

They chuckled for several more minutes at the image of Smythe in a state of self-generated anger, full of himself, muttering about the lesser beings in the world not understanding that when they were in his company they were in the company of greatness.

Eventually, Simpson turned serious and said to McAllister, "I have a request of you."

"Just tell me what it is," McAllister replied. "You know that I'll do anything I can to help you out."

"I just don't want to put you in a position where your job will be in jeopardy," Simpson said. "I can use your help with something I have to do, but if you think it will cause you any hardships at all, I'll completely understand if you can't do it."

"How about you tell me what you need, and let me decide if it

The Hypocrite

is something I can do?" McAllister answered.

"That meeting I told you about, the one scheduled for tomorrow night up at city hall? I would greatly appreciate it if you could see your way clear to joining us. I would really like your input on how it goes. Maybe you'll see something with a fresh set of eyes that we've missed. Maybe you can see a path out of this and by next spring we'll be all set for a ground-breaking."

McAllister didn't hesitate for an instant.

"I'll be there," he said.

"You don't have to speak or anything," Simpson added. "Just sit there in the audience, watch what happens and draw your own conclusions." He hesitated for a minute, and then asked McAllister, "How will you square this with your boss? He'll probably want to know why you suddenly showed up at something that has nothing to do with your job."

McAllister was quiet for a minute as well, and then a smile brightened his face. "I'll just tell him that I've been agonizing ever since I missed that lunch in July, and after hearing Lemming talking about the meeting on the phone I realized I found a way to redeem myself."

Simpson looked at McAllister for a long minute. His face was not unfriendly, but he obviously was confused at the same time.

Finally, he looked straight at McAllister and said in total sincerity, "You know, I really like you. You are the type of man who can be counted on, and who won't let his fellow man down. But frankly, I never know when you are being serious, or just pulling my leg."

McAllister smiled at the elder, "Neither do I," he replied. "But don't feel bad about it. I've had a lot more time to get to know me than you have. There's still hope."

"That's exactly what I'm talking about," Simpson said with a

The Hypocrite

chuckle as he started away. "Tomorrow night, then?"

"Tomorrow night," McAllister confirmed.

Shortly after Simpson left the cemetery, McAllister followed suit, driving back to the office. Once again, just after he pulled out of the cemetery, a dark sedan, looking very similar to Smythe's Lexus pulled out of the parking lot at the Center Tavern.

Once again it followed McAllister as he drove back to the office. But this time something was different, in that McAllister noticed the car behind him. He might have dismissed it as just circumstance, two similar looking cars, but this time the car had a blue and white sticker on the sun visor and small as it was, the sticker caught McAllister's attention.

Long ago a police detective told McAllister that, when he was on a case requiring surveillance, he did it in a nondescript car of a common and popular model with absolutely no identifying features, so it would not stand out. "There should be nothing remarkable that a subject will remember on that car," he said.

But this car had a sticker on the visor. McAllister saw it in Wethersfield, and he saw it again a few blocks from the office, always two cars behind him. The car turned off one block from the office, but McAllister noticed it, and remembered.

Neither Smythe nor Lemming was present, and McAllister went straight to his office, resuming work on Jamieson's account. He didn't see or hear either Smythe or the receptionist for the rest of the day, and at quitting time he finished his work, copied it to a file that he emailed to Smythe, copied it to his flash drive, put the flash drive in his pocket and headed home.

Julia was waiting for him as he entered the door. "How was your day?" she asked. "Were the other kids nice or were they mean at recess?"

The Hypocrite

"It was a Smythe day, as only Smythe days can be," McAllister replied. "Give me a minute and I'll fill you in." He started up the stairs to change, but stopped on the second tread, turning to Julia, "Hey, what are you doing tomorrow night? Want to go on a date?"

Chapter 9

Big Fish—Small Pond

The town hall was located—conveniently and appropriately—between Old Main Street and Church Street about a mile from the parcel where the elders hoped to construct their church.

Meetings of the zoning commission and related agencies normally would not draw much of a crowd and were held in one of several small meeting rooms elsewhere in the building designed especially for that purpose. But, tonight's meeting was in the chambers reserved for council meetings and larger gatherings. City officials wisely decided to use the council chambers, as a large crowd, composed primarily of church members and supporters, was gathering.

Bruce and Julia McAllister entered the room from the main entrance at the rear and were unnoticed as they found seats close to the door in the public seating section. McAllister recognized several elders from The Church of the Lord seated in the front row with family members.

Moran Smythe was in front of the first row of seats, standing with his back to the general public, but speaking in an animated fash-

The Hypocrite

ion to several other church members and some members of the Rocky Hill government. McAllister recognized some of the city officials because of the campaign flyers they had sent to Smythe's office before the last election—which were still in the reception area.

Smythe's voice could be heard, but McAllister could make out only brief snippets of the conversation—words such as "misunderstanding," and "clear the air," and "cooperation."

But it wasn't Smythe and his center-stage-grabbing antics that caught McAllister's attention. Rather, it was the look Smythe was getting from Derrick Simpson who was standing off to the side and slightly behind Smythe. While Smythe directed his attention to the town officials, Simpson was directing his attention to Smythe and his face was the same square-jawed, serious visage that McAllister remembered from their first encounter in the Center Cemetery back in July.

Julia was not familiar with any of the main players on the stage except by name and she occasionally leaned close to McAllister's ear, asking "Who is that?" as one or the other took the lead in the conversation at the front of the room. McAllister filled her in as best he could, identifying them by name and position.

He was turned toward Julia at one such point, just before the start of the meeting, when the door behind them opened noisily and in strode Lemming, her bright red hair sticking straight up from her head after she pulled off her cap without bothering to smooth it down. She appeared to have a halo of fire shooting out of her skull as she purposely headed toward the front of the room, looking neither left nor right, stopping at the second row of seats, directly behind the row where the elders were sitting. This night she also had added a swatch of bright red, garish-looking lipstick that went far outside the boundaries of her mouth. McAllister wondered if she had deliberately made herself up to look like a clown.

The Hypocrite

The second row on the right side of the room contained part of the overflow of church members and families, and there was one empty seat about three-quarters of the way over toward the wall. McAllister felt a momentary sense of anticipation as he waited to see the disruption Lemming would make as she squeezed her hefty frame between the back of the front row seats and the knees of those already sitting down in the second row.

"She just can't do anything without making a scene," he was thinking. But then Lemming went a step further.

"Move down," she commanded to the first church member in the aisle seat. "I'm not sitting way down there."

The member, a thirty-ish man with a solid build, dressed in business-casual—sport jacket and slacks, no tie—looked askance at Lemming as if he couldn't believe what he just heard.

"Move down!" Lemming commanded again, in a voice that carried throughout the room and brought unbelieving stares from the front row and the gathering of elders and officials still talking about the coming meeting. Smythe turned a fixed glare on the hapless church member, who reluctantly stood and asked quietly that everyone in the row up to the empty seat move down one spot.

They did, but the glares that were shot at both Lemming and Smythe were unkindly at best, possibly even un-Christian. Everyone finally was resettled, and Lemming sat triumphantly in the aisle seat, looking straight ahead and ignoring the glares and stares.

The group in the front broke up a few seconds later and Smythe took a seat directly in front of Lemming. He didn't look back over the crowd and thus didn't see McAllister. But Simpson did.

He caught McAllister's eye, nodded ever so slightly, which McAllister returned in kind, and then sat down. Julia, who had been watching the events at the front unfold, whispered just before the

The Hypocrite

meeting was called to order, "I don't have to guess the identity of the redhead, do I?"

McAllister shook his head no.

Suddenly realizing that the cast of characters as she knew it didn't appear complete, she asked, "Where's The Wife?"

"Not here," McAllister responded.

"Why?"

McAllister simply shrugged at Julia's last question because he had no answer.

The meeting was quickly called to order and the commission chairman asked the audience to stand and salute the flag. They recited the Pledge of Allegiance and then sat back down as the meeting began.

The minutes of the previous meeting were read and approved, and then the chairman asked for a motion to suspend the order of the agenda.

"We have a large gathering here tonight," he said, "and the rest of the business is fairly routine. There are no other individuals or groups on the agenda, so, if I can have a motion to suspend the agenda with the intent of moving the business of The Church of the Lord to the next item, we can expedite the process for everyone who came out tonight."

Another member responded, "So moved." The motion was seconded and it passed unanimously.

The chairman asked for an overview of the situation regarding the church building project, and that is where things at the meeting got interesting, not just for McAllister but for most of the congregation and other supporters.

A staff member from the zoning office, a pleasant looking young woman named Leona Williams, sitting at the far end of the row of commission members, took a sheaf of papers from a large manila fold-

The Hypocrite

er in front of her, and then addressed the meeting.

"Mr. Chairman, there appears to be a misunderstanding on the progress of the church's application for a building permit to construct a church on a parcel of land near Dividend Pond and Dividend Brook. The church has complied with all local zoning and wetlands regulations, and also has submitted the required data to the state and federal wetlands regulatory agencies, including the Environmental Protection Agency and the US Army Corps of Engineers.

"Both of those agencies have input and jurisdiction over the site in question," she added, "and because the parcel in question is near a wetlands, near the Connecticut River floodplain, and alongside a tributary of the Connecticut River, both agencies did review the application. Nonetheless, there is nothing about that particular parcel that makes it unbuildable because of the local topography.

"The land is large enough to accommodate construction of a building of this type, but for reasons that I have not been appraised of, the federal authorities have not signed off on the application. There are some issues regarding how and where measurements were taken regarding the setbacks from the pond and the stream, as well as associated wetlands.

"Nonetheless, having walked the property in question and made measurements of our own, it is the opinion of the staff that the property is in compliance. Frankly, we don't know why there is a delay and we have had no contact from state or federal authorities that would explain it."

The chairman thanked her for the review, and then called on Derrick Simpson to speak for the church.

Simpson rose, stood straight and tall, took a position to the right side of the commission's long table, and turned at a forty-five degree angle so he could address both the commission and the audience

The Hypocrite

simultaneously. Simpson was a public speaker with a long history of both formal education in the field, as well as years of addressing public gatherings, and he learned early in his career that, if you face as many people as possible, the risk of alienating someone sitting behind you is significantly reduced.

"Mr. Chairman, commission members, staff and members of the public," Simpson began. "The Church of the Lord has grown considerably in the past few years, and while we once were content with meeting in rented halls, we now would like to build our own church.

"We searched for quite some time to find a suitable parcel that fits both our worship needs and our community outreach efforts. We want to establish a soup kitchen for the needy and private counseling facilities for a myriad of social issues. Because we anticipate being active on more than just the Sabbath, we want a place that is accessible, yet not within an established neighborhood.

"We believe we found that spot, and are doing everything we have been asked by every agency—local, state, and federal—to comply with all the regulations and requirements. Yet, nearly a year has passed, and we seem to have an impasse, and worse, we can't find out what we need to do to move forward.

"So, I asked our town officials for this meeting tonight so we all can be in the same room at the same time and hash this out. As a church community we decided several months ago that we were in over our heads, so we authorized Mr. Smythe, a member of our church and our treasurer, to hire an attorney to work through the regulations for us. I understand that the attorney can't be with us tonight, and while we are tremendously disappointed at that, we still believe that, if we all communicate, we can figure out what needs to be done.

"Now, as I understand it, we have to be within 200 feet, measured horizontally, from the ordinary high water mark of Dividend

The Hypocrite

Brook or within 100 feet of wetlands associated with the brook. The issue appears to be that since we have a very steep slope on the side of the property that faces the brook, there is a disagreement on the measurements.

"We hired a surveyor last year and he believes that using both hard measurements from walking the property, and the application of a geometric model to the parcel taking the local terrain into account, we are in compliance. Yet, here we are with no permit to begin construction, winter right around the corner and no progress.

"So, if we are missing something or if our attorney hasn't been on target, we'd like to hear it tonight, so we can rectify whatever it is that is holding us back."

As Simpson was finishing he noticed that the commission chairman had left his seat and walked to the far end of the commission table to quietly speak with Williams and the other staff members seated there. Simpson stopped and looked straight at the chairman, who suddenly realized Simpson was finished and straightened up with a somewhat guilty look on his face.

"My apologies, Mr. Simpson," he said. "I wasn't being disrespectful. But the commission staff informs me that we have no record of meeting with any attorney who was representing your church. We agree with you that this seems like a misunderstanding that should be easily resolved, but we don't have any records of any inquiries regarding your project prior to your asking for tonight's meeting."

Simpson was seated by the time the commission chairman was midway through his comments, but when it was revealed that no lawyer was working with the commission staff, McAllister noticed Simpson's back stiffen.

There was no response for several seconds, then Simpson slowly stood again, addressing the chairman, but with an incredibly hard

The Hypocrite

look directed toward Smythe. "Since this was Moran Smythe's part of the project, and since he is here tonight, perhaps we should hear directly from him."

Simpson again took his seat and the chairman nodded in concurrence. "Mr. Smythe?" he said.

Smythe slowly stood, and after a pause during which he stared at the members of the commission individually, he glanced over his shoulder in the general direction of the public with a smug acknowledgement of their existence.

"I am Moran Smythe," he began, "and I'm certain you all know me."

McAllister barely had time to absorb the egotism of that statement, when a wit in the audience called out just loud enough for all in the chambers to hear, "Who?"

McAllister and Julia agreed later that night that they both saw a deep red flush creeping quickly up the back of Smythe's neck, a sure sign that he didn't see the humor in the previous comment—although just about everyone else in the room did, judging by the repressed laughter.

"I am Moran Smythe." The statement was made loudly and forcibly. Smythe was not a happy camper.

"My family was among the founders of the neighboring community of Wethersfield when Connecticut was barely a colony. My ancestors were members of the business community, church-going farmers and merchants, and it was by their hard work, perseverance and foresight that a significant contribution was made to the success of the colony.

"My ancestors not only were instrumental in the success of Wethersfield, but when the colonists began moving south and east, the Smythe name was among them. We were settlers of Rocky Hill, as

The Hypocrite

well as Glastonbury across the river, when they were still part of the community of Wethersfield.

"We have a centuries-old history of being good stewards of our form of government, our church, and the land on which we still do our business. We have been contributing members of this community literally for centuries, and what I have heard here tonight is an abomination!"

Smythe's voice went up several decibels in loudness—as well as several octaves—as he spoke and there was an audible gasp from the audience when he said "abomination."

In truth, right up to that instant the proceedings were cordial, and there was a sense among the members of the congregation that the elders were making real headway in resolving the roadblock to their project for the first time in many months.

If anyone in the room understood why Smythe was so upset and getting more so with every passing second, it probably was only Smythe himself, although Lemming was dutifully nodding her assent as Smythe's speech progressed.

"I have been working diligently for months now to find out exactly why our application process is stalled. I have personally met with our legal representatives on numerous occasions on my own time and at my own expense, but now you tell me you have never heard from the man!" Smythe was literally thundering, and he looked as though his head would explode at any second.

"We have been patient, we have been thorough, and we have complied with everything that has been asked of us. We have hired legal counsel, surveyors and land use experts to help guide us through this process and now you tell us there are no records of our attorney's efforts? This is appalling!"

Smythe paused to take a breath, and the chairman used that

The Hypocrite

space to ask a question that was on everyone's mind. "Mr. Smythe, could you give us the name of your legal counsel? It is possible the record of his visits or correspondence has been misfiled. If so, we can find out with a simple computer search of our database."

"Absolutely NOT!" Smythe thundered again. "I have no authority to speak on his behalf or about him in public. I will check with him tomorrow, get his version of this issue and contact the commission staff when I have an opportunity."

But the chairman persisted. "Mr. Smythe, we are trying to help here. It won't hurt to get his name. Perhaps we can contact him in the morning and he can help fill in the blanks here. I'm sure it is just a matter of communicating with each other."

Smythe glared down at the chairman and the rest of the commission members in turn. "I am Moran Smythe, and I have spoken." The words came out clipped, but at times nearly a hiss, as from an angry snake.

"How dare you question me?" he shot at the chairman and then, without a further word, turned on his heel and stalked toward the exit. Or, more accurately, he tried to stalk toward the exit. But, while the swelling in his lip and mouth, incurred the day of his tryst with Lemming was gone, his limp was still evident. Smythe had endured only several days of slurred speech due to hitting his mouth on his desk, but the injury to his knee still bothered him. While he tried to appear powerful, majestic even, as he left the meeting, he still couldn't disguise the painful limp. He looked neither left nor right, but as soon as he passed Lemming's chair his grand exit went from bad to worse. Lemming dutifully rose, shot a withering look at the commission, with a special 'I hate you' look for the staff, and followed quickly on Smythe's heels.

McAllister thought he was going to escape notice, not that he cared, but he didn't need any more of the office drama when he went to work in the morning. However, it was not to be. Smythe caught sight of McAllister and Julia and was so shocked his head nearly snapped off his neck.

Smythe even lost a half-step, looking for an instant as though he was going to stop in mid-stride. Lemming, who was right behind him, bumped into Smythe, who shot forward, losing what he thought was his righteous exit from the chambers, appearing even more bumbling and confused instead.

They burst out the exit door like a comedy duo in a silent era slapstick, and some members of the audience couldn't help but laughing. Smythe heard them and his anger increased exponentially, but he didn't return to the council chambers.

Simpson already was standing by the time Smythe and Lemming left the room, and when the door closed he turned back to face the Zoning Commission.

"Mr. Chairman, I feel it is my duty to apologize," Simpson said with great formality. "I believe, and I'm sure my brethren will back me up, that the commission and its staff are trying to help us resolve this issue. Mr. Smythe was talking for himself, not our church. We won't take any more of your time on this. I'll be in contact with the staff as soon as I unravel all this mystery."

The chairman, who was still feeling the shock of Smythe's eruption, nodded to Simpson, then said simply, "I'll entertain a motion to return to the prepared agenda."

He heard a "so moved," asked for and received a second, then another unanimous vote to proceed with business.

The commission members sat silently as the audience departed. McAllister and Julia could have been among the first people out the door, but they waited until Derrick Simpson came near and then

The Hypocrite

moved out into the aisle next to him.

Simpson had the look of a very worried man, and spoke sparingly to McAllister.

"We have to talk," was all he said.

"Say when and where," was McAllister's response.

"I'll be in touch," Simpson told him and the conversation ended there.

They moved out into the hallway heading toward the exit, still walking side by side with Julia on the outside away from Simpson. McAllister intended to introduce his wife to Simpson but then, all things considered, decided against it, preferring to wait for a better time.

They were nearing the outside exit when another man sidled up alongside Simpson, matching him stride for stride. The newcomer was smaller than either Simpson or McAllister, looked to be in his mid to late forties, bookish, in that he had thinning hair and wire rimmed spectacles.

"It wasn't like that you know," he said to Simpson. "What Smythe said about his family wasn't like that at all."

"What do you mean?"

"I mean his family didn't help found Wethersfield or Rocky Hill. My name is Harold Turner, I'm a member of the Historical Society, and a few years ago, I did some research after hearing Smythe go off like that at another meeting.

"The records from back then are pretty scarce but from what I could find, his ancestors were literally driven out of Wethersfield for drunkenness and dishonesty. They weren't big on religion, either.

"There was some information in the old town records about the original Smythe owning a tavern up there by the green somewhere, but it burned down just before they left town.

The Hypocrite

"When the old pole ferry first went into service around 1655, the Smythe's got work as pole men working for the families that actually ran it. When poles gave way to a rope the Smythe's worked as laborers, pulling on the rope that propelled the boat back and forth to the shore in Glastonbury, until they were replaced by a horse on a treadmill."

"They really didn't do much of anything for generations except exist and occasionally get into trouble. He wouldn't even be the big noise he is in town, but his wife brought along a lot of money when they married. That business originally belonged to her father. Smythe inherited it and changed the name after her father died. That death was mysterious too, if you get my meaning."

Simpson took it all in stride, finally saying only, "Thank you. That will be very helpful I'm sure."

Turner moved away then and they continued out into the November night, no one saying anything. It was only a week until Thanksgiving, and the cold November air was delivering the first bites of the coming winter. McAllister pulled his coat tighter and asked Julia if she was warm enough. She merely nodded, lost in her own thoughts as was nearly everyone else that night.

Simpson walked off toward his vehicle without saying anything else. McAllister couldn't help but feel sorry for him. Derrick Simpson was a good man, living his life in the way he thought best. He was a straight arrow, and McAllister had seen numerous instances of helpfulness and kindness from him. There also was an air about Simpson that led McAllister to believe that he was not a man to be trifled with.

They arrived at the truck and McAllister unlocked the passenger side for Julia, closing the door behind her when she was settled into the seat. Then he went to his side, got in, started the truck and put the heater on, waiting for the engine to get warm. He made no effort to

The Hypocrite

leave, preferring to let the other traffic go first.

The streets of Rocky Hill were all but deserted even though it wasn't even 8:30 p.m. The traffic exited the town hall parking lot quickly and McAllister finally put the truck in gear and headed for the street.

"It's still early," he finally said to Julia. "Would you like to stop somewhere for a drink and a debriefing?"

Julia wrinkled her nose at his use of military terminology, but answered, "By debriefing do you mean you want to take my clothes off? In public?" McAllister began laughing and Julia didn't wait for an answer. "Yes, that would be nice, I think. Not over on this side of the river though. Let's get closer to home."

McAllister agreed. "There are a couple of nice places in Glastonbury. Pick one and we'll go there."

"Give me a minute," Julia answered. Then she slid across the seat, as far as her seat belt would allow, and put her head on his shoulder.

"Are you okay?" McAllister asked with a strong note of concern in his voice.

"I'm fine," Julia answered. "But I was just thinking," she added, slipping her hand over McAllister's knee, "you really know how to show a girl a good time."

Chapter 10

We Still Don't Know You
(The Elders are Worried)

"The meeting will come to order!"

Derrick Simpson, seated at the center of an eight-foot table, rapped his gavel to get the attention of the three-dozen people packed into the meeting room facing him. The table top was cream colored, and constructed from a composite material that provided a solid report when the wood of his gavel struck it.

The table had folding legs for easy transport and storage, and was an inexpensive yet durable piece of furniture that was purchased three years earlier at a national discount chain store. It served the congregation of The Church of the Lord very well and only a week ago seated ten people at the monthly pot-luck dinner.

Tonight it was set up at the front of a basement room in a large farm-style home belonging to church member Will Morton. Simpson rapped his gavel again for emphasis and the low-level conversation in the room ended quickly. The few people who were standing took seats in the folding chairs that were set up for this meeting.

Moran Smythe's outburst on Thursday night was the focal point

The Hypocrite

of nearly all church-related conversations in the past two days. People were concerned, upset, somewhat afraid of what he could do to the congregation's reputation, and most of all they wanted to know what was happening to their plans for a building—and the money they had provided to Smythe for legal services.

Simpson spent a great part of the day Friday on the phone with the elders and other parishioners deciding what they should do after the meeting at Town Hall Thursday night. All agreed that it was a fiasco, a huge embarrassment for the church, and raised a host of new questions while providing no answers.

Ultimately they decided to meet on Saturday night so the issues could be discussed and some consensus reached before the Sabbath. The elders chose not to invite Moran Smythe, putting it to a vote in a near-unanimous decision, and agreeing the meeting would be held out of town in the hopes that Smythe would not stumble onto it by accident.

Tonight's meeting had a number of goals. First was to provide an opportunity to vent the frustrations felt by nearly everyone, second to formulate both immediate and long-term future plans, and third to give parishioners the opportunity to speak freely without the presence of Moran Smythe looming over their shoulders.

They were gathered in Newington, a town adjacent to Rocky Hill, in Morton's spacious home. Morton was both a member of the church and an elder. He lived in a century-old farmhouse where his family still raised beef cattle on twenty-five acres of adjacent land.

His basement was completely modernized several years earlier and often served as a meeting place for social groups as well as a gathering point for his extended family, especially on Sundays after church. Simpson asked Morton to hold the meeting there on Saturday night due to its spaciousness and the concerns expressed by so many of the

The Hypocrite

members—that if Smythe found out about the meeting he might crash it, or worse, take out his anger on individual church members when they were alone.

Upon review, Smythe's membership in the church reflected a mixture of early good wishes and more recent resentment. He was a welcome addition when he first showed up about five years previously, but that didn't last long. Simpson, who was tending to his ailing wife and then dealing with her untimely death, was an elder at that time, but most of his attention was understandably focused on issues in his home. He was aware that Smythe joined their ranks, but most of the initial input he received from other parishioners was positive.

In the early days, parishioners saw Smythe as a sizable and vocal champion of the evangelistic viewpoint, who could and would intimidate critics or others who thought that being an evangelist meant wearing a target on one's back. He rose quickly in the church hierarchy, and became an elder pretty much because he said so. But it didn't take long for parishioners to realize that Smythe could be just as intimidating toward other members of the church, who had the temerity to disagree with him, as he could on outsiders. It started out with small things and involved only one or two people, but over time Smythe managed to alienate an increasingly large segment of the congregation.

Other parishioners were intent on doing good works, and were spreading their message far and wide, with the expected result of increasing the numbers of people showing up for Sunday services. Many of those who came for Sunday services began joining other activities such as Bible study, dinners and community outreach. But even as the membership grew, Smythe seemed bent on making the point to one and all that he was the ultimate authority on matters of Christianity, as McAllister had found out soon after he began his employment at

The Hypocrite

Smythe Partners, Ltd. The unfortunate result was a growing number of potential members who decided to apply their faith elsewhere after running head-first into a dispute with Smythe.

Most people who clashed with Smythe ended up capitulating or just not responding, not because they agreed with him or were convinced by his arguments, but because he could become physically threatening and most people don't go to church to get into a fight. But for all his bombast and bullying, Smythe made a major blunder in his relationships with the elders and church members. He underestimated them for starters, and he completely misunderstood the basis for their actions, factors that were first noticed by none other than Derrick Simpson.

In the months and then years after the death of his wife, as Simpson gradually began to get his grief under control, he returned to a more active role in the church, becoming the senior elder, as much by his own leadership style as by universal agreement of the congregation. His input was sought on matters large and small, which ultimately brought him into direct contact, and often conflict, with Smythe. Smythe didn't like Simpson from the beginning, probably because he saw Simpson as a threat, but he underestimated Simpson as much as he underestimated the rest of the congregation.

Smythe claimed to be an evangelist, but he was surprisingly short on both the knowledge and character associated with that title. When a parishioner with whom he was having a disagreement finally gave up and walked away, Smythe saw that action as weakness and acquiescence to his point of view. He seemed to be ignorant of the fact that the people he was bullying were devout followers of Jesus Christ, and as such they were not inclined to violence. They were intent on spreading the message of hope and joy and life everlasting. Being the best arm wrestler in church was not part of the equation.

The Hypocrite

But there was a limit to most parishioners' tolerance. They were non-violent—to a point. They believed in turning the other cheek—to a point. Smythe had long since pushed most of the parish membership way past that point, but he was so absorbed in his own view of himself and his power that he didn't see the signs of unrest and discontent.

Smythe's arrogance and bullying formed part of the evening's agenda, but only part. As the room became quiet Simpson briefly outlined the purpose of the meeting, and acknowledged three other elders seated with him at the table. To his left was the recording secretary, a pleasant woman named Mildred who was born in the south and raised a Southern Baptist.

She had moved north more than a decade ago and quickly established herself in The Church of the Lord. She became the church secretary by default and acclimation, when it was revealed that she not only could take notes, but was adept at Gregg's shorthand—once a staple of public education for young women, but nearly forgotten these days. Mildred wore her honey colored hair in a bun and used reading glasses when she was taking notes. She spoke in a southern drawl that was as soft as the color of her hair, but Simpson learned early on that she had a mind like a steel trap and determination to match.

To Simpson's immediate right was Jonathon Anderson, a slight black man with an affinity for musical instruments and a terrific baritone voice. Anderson taught music at a private high school and was anxious for the day when the congregation could build its own church and build a proper choir.

He was proficient on several musical instruments including the piano, organ and saxophone and loved impromptu songfests, leaning heavily toward traditional hymns and Christian rock. Anderson also had a well-developed sense of humor and was a great conciliator, a man who could calm the troubled waters of personal relationships

The Hypocrite

and bring a smile to faces that only moments earlier were locked in a frown. But he didn't like Smythe.

Seated next to Anderson was Chris Gaston, a tank of a man, six-feet tall, 220 pounds, most of it muscle and one of the few members of the church who was not the least bit cowed by Smythe. Smythe knew it too and avoided Gaston like the plague. Despite his size and formidable demeanor, Gaston was a quiet man who spoke with great deliberation and calmness. But like the others in the church, Gaston had his limits.

In his earlier years, Gaston was an Army Ranger and served several tours in Vietnam. He was skilled at various forms of martial arts and it generally was not considered a good idea to make a habit of irritating him just to see what might happen. He did not like Smythe either, and despite his unshakeable belief that his religion was inclusive, and that those who needed it most could benefit from it the most, he long ago had reached the point where he no longer believed Smythe should be a member of the congregation.

Simpson acknowledged the elders at the table and the others who were scattered throughout the rest of the room. He asked that the congregation stand and start the meeting with a prayer, which they did. They intoned Amen in unison, and then Simpson got down to business.

"We're here tonight to discuss the situation regarding Brother Smythe. Many of you attended the meeting in Town Hall Thursday night where we were supposed to get an explanation and update on our application for a building permit to construct our church.

"For those of you who were not there, it was not a pleasant evening for us, and rather than answer our concerns, a number of new questions have been raised. First among these is whether we have a lawyer, even though this congregation anted up $35,000 last summer

The Hypocrite

specifically to pay for legal assistance and related costs.

"But at the meeting Thursday, the zoning office staffers said they hadn't been contacted by a lawyer representing us, and when they asked Smythe for a name, he went off on a tangent, yelling about how his family settled this town and how dare they question him! Then he and Gail Lemming stalked out of the meeting leaving us holding the bag.

"The good news is that the staff thinks there is just a miscommunication at the federal level that should be easily resolved. But so far, it doesn't appear that anyone has been told there is a problem, and therefore nothing has been done to resolve it. So, tonight, I would like to hear from anyone who has input on this situation and once we've had our say, then we need to come to a consensus on where we go from here.

"Who would like to speak?"

At first the room was silent and no one raised a hand. Then after a few uncomfortable seconds, a woman near the back spoke up.

"Derrick, I'd like to be heard if I may."

"Of course, Shirley, please have your say."

Shirley rose from her seat and started, hesitantly at first. "When Moran Smythe first joined us I thought it was great. He was outgoing, he wasn't the least bit afraid to speak his mind to others—and I know that at one time or another we have all been the targets of people who don't think as we do.

"But, after a while I began to see him in a different light. He always has to be right, even in discussions where there is no right or wrong—just interpretations. I began to see him abusing people verbally and walking in real close, getting his face right in theirs, about things that really didn't mean much.

"I have seen him time after time pushing our men around, using

The Hypocrite

his size to get his way when his arguments wouldn't work. I see him look at women as if they are his toys, not real people with real feelings and beliefs."

Shirley paused momentarily, but remained standing.

"Is that it, Shirley?" Simpson asked gently.

"No," she replied, "there's one more thing. I have been trying to decide whether I should say this or not, but I think it should be out in the open." Shirley paused again, and then blurted out, "I just can't stand the way he treats his wife. That poor woman looks so sad and so dejected every time I see her. If he acts the way he does in public, what on earth does he do to her in private? We don't even know her name. He just calls her The Wife. It's embarrassing for us as Christians and it's embarrassing for our community. And it is just plain wrong. It breaks my heart to see the sadness in her eyes."

Others at the meeting were nodding in agreement as Shirley poured out her frustration with Smythe, but her final statement about The Wife brought a chorus of "Amen!" It was a strong showing of the frustration in the room and a harbinger of the remainder of the evening.

Shirley was finished and sat down to hearty applause. Following her, speaker after speaker stood and gave a similar version of events they had experienced or had seen involving Smythe. Not one speaker had a good thing to say. Everyone was of the opinion that he put his best foot forward until he was accepted into the church, and from that point on the true Smythe was revealed.

Simpson knew the speakers were going beyond redundancy but he allowed the discussion to continue as long as someone had something to say. The frustration was palpable and Simpson figured it was better to let the parishioners vent than to keep the issue bottled up. Essentially Smythe was regarded as an egotistical, self-absorbed, myopic,

The Hypocrite

insulting, arrogant, condescending know-it-all who was all too willing to let people think he would become physical if he were challenged.

After a dozen more speakers told their version of Smythe's bullying, Simpson called on a member sitting in the back of the room, who thus far had remained quiet, not even resorting to nodding in agreement. Simpson noticed the man's hand raised to shoulder height, as though he wasn't sure of what he wanted to say. "Malcolm, do you have something you want to add?"

Malcolm was an average-looking man, of average height and average weight. In fact, people often remarked that if you weren't looking directly at him, it would be difficult to give an accurate description of Malcolm. But he also was known as a man, who on occasion, could be thoughtful and deliberate and his opinions usually were valued. But Malcolm also had a darker side, a seething sense of jealously against anyone who didn't understand just how important he was in the world. He was average, but he was not weak. In fact his stature disguised a hidden strength, and worse, he was really a classic bully who could be vicious to those who were smaller and weaker than he.

Malcolm stood as the others before him had, but embarked on a different track. "I know that what everyone else has said is true," he started out, "partly because I have seen many of the same things myself. But I also think I should remind my friends and neighbors that we are a Christian organization, and frankly, some of the things I have been hearing tonight don't sound very Christian.

"We are supposed to be loving, and kind, and forgiving. We are supposed to believe in the concept that 'vengeance is mine sayeth the Lord.' But I don't feel much love or much forgiveness here tonight. What I do feel is a desire for vengeance. I don't think it is our role or our responsibility to do the work here on earth that the Lord will do in the Hereafter."

The Hypocrite

Malcolm sat down and the room was silent.

Simpson asked if anyone else wished to speak, but there were no takers.

"Why don't we take a ten-minute break before we get to the next phase of the meeting," Simpson said. "If you didn't see it on the way in, the table in back has some snacks, sodas, coffee and juice. We'll reconvene in ten minutes."

The sound of chairs scraping on the floor filled the room and a line quickly formed at the refreshment table. Simpson leaned back in his chair and watched, as Anderson and Gaston walked to the back of the room.

Mildred remained seated next to Simpson at the table, going over her notes and marking certain spots where she might need to revise the wording.

"What do you think of Malcolm's input?" Simpson asked her.

"He certainly does a good job of reminding us who we are and where our priorities are supposed to be," she answered. Then she added, "Bless his heart," in a slow southern drawl that could easily have been dripping with molasses.

Simpson couldn't help but laugh out loud at that, and Mildred did her best to keep from doing the same. When Mildred first came to the church and used the phrase 'Bless His (or her) Heart,' everyone thought it was a statement of kindness or praise.

But after she got to know Simpson, and was sure she could trust him, Mildred confided that the phrase wasn't a compliment at all, but a synonym for "Dummy" or words of similar meaning. So, when she said, "Bless His Heart" about Malcolm speaking up on Smythe's behalf, she certainly wasn't agreeing with him, nor for that matter, speaking kindly of his point of view.

Simpson watched as the line at the refreshment table dwindled

The Hypocrite

and when nearly everyone was headed back to the chairs, he went to the back and poured himself a cup of decaf coffee, adding a good dose of half-n-half. As he stirred the cream he looked through the window on the entrance door and saw a set of headlights out on the street, going by very slowly, as if looking for an address or parking spot.

The driveway overflowed with parishioners' cars and more lined the street for yards on both sides. Simpson decided as he returned to the head table that he would wait a few more minutes to reconvene the meeting in case of a late arrival. Five minutes later, he decided the passing car was just being careful and called the meeting to order again.

But the car outside was not just a passing neighbor. It was a black Lexus, and it actually passed four times, going very slowly each time. Inside the car a very agitated Moran Smythe was beside himself with anger. "Think they're smart do they? Think they can pull a fast one on me, do they? We'll see!"

On his third pass, Smythe parked at the end of the line of cars, exited his vehicle with a notebook and pen in hand, and walked slowly along the line, stopping at each vehicle and making notes in his booklet. He even walked part way up the drive, listing the vehicles parked there. When he was finished Smythe returned to the Lexus, started it, turned around and drove away. His anger was barely under control, and Smythe repeatedly smashed his fist on the steering wheel.

As he drove back toward Rocky Hill, Smythe briefly considered going to the bar in Wethersfield but decided instead to go straight home. She didn't know it yet, but The Wife was in for a very long and very unpleasant night.

Simpson had returned to his seat and didn't see the lights from Smythe's vehicle as it made repeated passes outside. The meeting was already back in progress by the time Smythe left the area. Simpson

The Hypocrite

began the next phase by addressing Malcolm and his previous comments.

"Malcolm, I appreciate the concern and the caution behind your statements. And it is always good to remind ourselves of our primary reason for existing, and our goals as a Christian community.

"We have heard from our friends and neighbors too, and their words are equally heartfelt. Basically, with the exception of Malcolm's comments," Simpson said to the gathering, "it is evident that nearly everyone here believes Moran Smythe is arrogant, self-absorbed, bombastic, insulting and abusive. I agree with Malcolm that those are not the kind of adjectives we Christians normally use when talking about another member of our congregation."

Malcolm was literally beaming by now, but his demeanor changed drastically in just a few more seconds.

"But, we are dealing with more than personality defects this evening," Simpson continued. "We are looking at possible fraud and larceny. As we all know stealing is a violation of one of the Ten Commandments. Thus, we have a moral dilemma. Should we confront Smythe, give him a chance to repent and let him off, or do we confront Smythe and then go to the authorities?"

Simpson paused for a half-minute, letting his words sink in. "It would be easy to forgive and forget. Just let God handle this in His own way and own time," he continued. "But, we have a greater moral responsibility than just to ourselves. What happens if we let this slide and down the road he steals from someone else? Won't we be morally culpable for the misfortunes of others?

"And while I think of it, wouldn't we be legally complicit if we knew Smythe stole from us and said nothing of it?"

The grumbling from the parishioners was a clear indication that they were not in a mood to let Smythe off the hook, Christian or not.

The Hypocrite

If anything, once their own issues were raised in public the animosity toward Smythe took on a life of its own and the consensus was that he should be gone—facing criminal charges if he stole church money.

Once again, Malcolm raised his hand, tentatively, but still, it was up.

"Yes, Malcolm?"

"Derrick, I understand the way everyone feels, but I have to ask, do we actually have any evidence that Moran stole from us, or didn't hire a lawyer? All I have heard so far is complaints about his character, but I haven't heard one word that would constitute evidence that he did anything illegal, or even immoral."

"That's true, we don't have any concrete evidence," Simpson admitted. "But, I intend to keep searching. And I suggest that we hold another meeting, with Moran in attendance this time, and give him the opportunity to invite the lawyer to meet with us, or at least show us the invoices for nearly five months of time spent on our case."

There was a sea of nods of assent, and then from the end of the table Gaston spoke up.

"Derrick, how about that young man that works for Smythe, Bruce McAllister? Do you think he might have any information that could shed some light on this? And if so, would he share it?"

Simpson didn't answer for a full minute, looking down at his hands which were folded on the table. Finally, he responded, "Bruce McAllister is a good person. He works hard, he is honest, and I personally witnessed Smythe giving him the type of abuse we heard about here tonight, which frankly I doubt McAllister would tolerate if he didn't need the job."

This time Malcolm shot right up out of his seat. "Who is this McAllister? Is he a member of our church? Is he planning on becoming a member of our church? I would remind you all, that Moran Smythe IS a member of our church and as Elder Simpson admitted

The Hypocrite

just a few minutes ago, we have absolutely no evidence that a man who has a history of contributing so much to our beliefs and our community has done anything wrong! Are you asking this McAllister person to spy on Moran Smythe? Are you?"

"First," Simpson responded, "I am not asking anyone to spy for us. I am just trying to get to the heart of this matter and any viable information that we can get from any source is welcome. And no, McAllister is not a member of our church nor has he indicated that he wants to join.

"He got out of the military a year or so ago, and I would have to say he is conflicted. He seems to be heading in the right direction and I have seen nothing from him that would cause me to question his character or his intents. But at the moment he isn't interested in making any commitments to us, or our church."

"Conflicted? What does that mean, 'conflicted?'" Malcolm was on his feet again, but this time his voice went up a couple of octaves and his tone was insistent, sounding very much like the tone Smythe used when someone was questioning him. "Moran Smythe isn't conflicted. He is not only sure of his beliefs, he is positive about them! And we are going to take the word of a non-believer who you described as 'conflicted' over that of a loyal member of our church?"

Before Simpson could respond Gaston spoke up again. "I'll handle this, Derrick," he said, with a voice as hard as tempered steel.

"I'll explain 'conflicted' to you Malcolm," he said, looking straight at, or possibly straight through, the parishioner who appeared to be Smythe's only ally in the room.

"McAllister is less than a year out of war, a war against terrorists in which the only rules are imposed on our fighters while the other side exults in having no restrictions at all. In fact the more brutal they are, the higher the esteem they are held in.

The Hypocrite

"He has come home from the most dehumanizing experience I can think of—a level of brutality that most people back here in our safe environment can't even begin to comprehend, and it will take him some time to wind down. He will need time to think about it without someone else telling him how he should be thinking. He will need time to sleep without always keeping one eye open, waiting for the attacks that always came in the darkest part of the night.

"He will need time to mourn his friends and conclude for himself whether their sacrifices were necessary." Gaston had been staring straight at Malcolm, who dropped his eyes to the floor before the first sentence was finished, and now was still staring down.

"Some of you may be aware that long ago I fought in Vietnam," Gaston said. "But you probably don't know that I came home from that war conflicted too. I've heard that McAllister questions why the chaplains who went there to minister to the troops never spoke up about the asinine Rules of Engagement that no sane person can follow. Or why they never went to the media when we needed more troops, while the politicians were jawing away back in Washington.

"I understand his conflicts because once I had the very same conflicts. And I'll tell you something else. If, after all that man has gone through—three tours in Iraq, major battles in each tour—he is a supporter of our right to have our beliefs and to worship as we see fit unmolested by either society or the government, then he is an ally, and I for one would appreciate his help in resolving this issue. He isn't being asked to spy on anyone, but if he has information that would work one way or the other, I think he would be a tremendous asset as a corroborating witness.

"Maybe someday he will join us, and maybe not, but either way we have done our job as evangelists. We have spread the word and he has heard it. What he does with it is up to him. It is not our place to

The Hypocrite

pressure him unduly, especially when he still needs time to decompress from his time in the Marines.

"And I'll conclude with this thought. Membership in our church is good, of course, but it is not the only criterion by which a person's worth is determined. Membership here does not automatically confer sainthood on our members."

Gaston stopped at that point and the room was completely silent.

Simpson cleared his throat and then said quietly, "I have nothing to add to that Chris. Does anyone else?"

No one spoke, except Anderson who said in a very low voice, "Amen, Brother."

Simpson decided it was time to bring the meeting to a conclusion. "I will contact McAllister and see if he has any information that can help us. Early next week I'll confer with the other elders and we'll set a date for another meeting. We'll invite Brother Smythe to the next one and try to get this all behind us.

"Please stand for our closing prayer."

The congregation stood for the benediction and at the end said, "Amen," in unison. "I'll see you tomorrow at our services," Simpson said. "Meeting adjourned."

Most of the men stood and immediately began clearing the room. They folded the chairs and took them to the truck of a member who would return them to a storage shed behind his house where they would be kept until the next event. The table went with them.

There was some milling around, as though the business part of the meeting was over but there was still much on people's minds. No one seemed to notice that Malcolm left the meeting immediately, muttering a few "good nights" on his way out the door, when it would have been obviously rude to do otherwise, but generally not speaking.

The Hypocrite

His car was on the street and he entered quickly, starting it and heading back to Rocky Hill without waiting. Before he had gone 100 yards he had his cell phone in his hand, clicking on his Contacts list. Toward the bottom of the alphabetical list was an entry for Smythe (home.)

Malcolm had the number on speed dial. He selected it, and hit Send.

Chapter 11

Decision Day at the Cemetery

Bruce McAllister was engaged in his favorite Sunday afternoon activity—at least in the fall.

Securely ensconced in his recliner chair, with a cooler containing two beers, two bottles of water and two diet sodas on ice by his side, a platter with crackers, sliced sharp cheddar cheese, pepperoni, chips and peanuts on the stand next to him, he was watching the Green Bay Packers and Chicago Bears football teams fight it out in Lambeau Field.

McAllister was raised on the east coast and his favorite team would be playing in the 4 p.m. time slot, but he also had a "second-tier of favorite teams," as he called them, which he knew would always provide a first-rate football game. Today, two of those teams faced off in the 1 p.m. time slot.

This game was all he expected and McAllister was thoroughly enjoying it. They went into the half-time show with the score tied at fourteen, and McAllister stood up and stretched, taking a moment to look out the window at the now barren landscape.

The Hypocrite

It was the Sunday before Thanksgiving and the ground was slowly freezing in preparation for the coming winter, with the snow and ice storms that surely were in the immediate future. It seemed unseasonably cold this year but the weather forecasters on the local news shows repeatedly assured their audiences that the temperatures were "normal."

McAllister turned at the sound of the telephone ringing, and checking the caller ID, saw that it was Derrick Simpson. He picked up the receiver and said, "Hello Derrick," hoping immediately after he said it that it really was Derrick and not someone else using his phone.

"Ah, the wonders of caller ID," he heard Simpson say on the other end. "Watching the Bears and Packers?"

"Yes, as a matter of fact I am," McAllister replied. "How did you know?"

"You told me once when we were over at the cemetery that you liked football in the fall and if I ever need you on a Sunday afternoon that's where I could find you. I figured the Chicago/Green Bay game was the better of the two that are on, and to be fair, I waited until halftime just in case you were really into it."

"Well, that was an astute observation on your part, Derrick. I do appreciate the consideration. So, what's going on?"

"We had a meeting last night," Simpson responded. "We, meaning the elders and some other parishioners who wanted to provide some input, but minus Moran Smythe. In fact, the subject of the meeting was Smythe and the way he behaved and spoke Thursday night."

"It was quite a show, wasn't it?" McAllister said. "I thought it was over the top, even for Smythe."

"A lot of other people agree with you," Simpson continued.

The Hypocrite

"By the way, did he have anything to say on Friday about your attendance?"

"As a matter of fact, he did," McAllister said. "But it wasn't as much or as intense as I expected. He just stuck his head in my office and asked why I was there. I told him exactly what I said to you last week—that I felt bad about missing the meeting in July and I thought maybe I could be of some help."

"How did he take that?" Simpson asked.

"He wanted to know how I found out about it, so I said I heard Lemming talking to someone on the phone when I was getting coffee. He muttered something about Lemming needing to watch her mouth, and he almost left it at that, but this was really strange. The last thing he said was, that if I wasn't at work I'd be wise to stay on the east side of the Connecticut River! Then he just walked out."

Simpson was silent for a few seconds then wondered aloud, "Why would he say something as irrelevant as that?"

"Well, there are some people, especially those who are terribly insecure, who tend to see the west side of the river as the well-to-do side, while on my side, I guess, we're supposed to be Neanderthals. From my point of view, paying hundreds of thousands of dollars for a buildable piece of land, that has neither the space, nor the view, nor the lower taxes that I pay isn't a wise expenditure, especially in this economy. But, why should I get in between a person and their sense of denial?"

Simpson chuckled at that. "I've always liked it over there, but of course I never saw it as 'over there' as opposed to just identifying the towns by name. Your part of the state is a beautiful place to go for a Sunday drive, what with the dairy farms and orchards, and a couple of really nice wineries, by the way."

"I agree with that," McAllister replied. "But there's more to

The Hypocrite

it than that for me. I enjoy the solitude when I want it, the lack of heavy traffic twenty four hours a day, the room to plant a garden and some fruit trees in my own yard, and even the wildlife. We have deer around all year, hawks, bald eagles, coyotes—which of course are a dangerous nuisance, but they're in the cities too. I can walk into my backyard to see wildlife if I want to, and I can fish for trout or bass or perch or pike in a dozen places within twenty minutes of my house."

"So how does East of the River qualify as somehow less than West of the River?" Simpson inquired.

"Like I said, only in the minds of some very insecure people," McAllister answered. "I mean, I get the concept of living in the city if that is what you like. But I can get a great meal at places serving anything from hot dogs, burgers or shakes to a four-star French restaurant. In fact, when Julia and I got engaged that is exactly where we went—the French restaurant I mean. There is great pizza, lots of ethnic options, just about anything you'll find in a city, but you have to drive a bit to get there. But enough of that. What happened at your meeting?"

"Basically, people want to know who the lawyer is that Smythe hired, if he actually hired someone. They also want to know how the $35,000 was spent. This is a pretty forgiving group of people. We try to practice what we preach. But we have our limits. They want receipts and I agree with them.

"I'm not going to take up your whole afternoon with this," Simpson concluded. "But do me a favor if you don't mind. Think back over the summer, and see if you remember anything that looked out of the ordinary, expenditure wise. And while you're at it, it would help if you ever saw Smythe meeting with someone who could be a lawyer. How about if we meet at the cemetery for lunch on Tuesday, and we can talk some more?"

The Hypocrite

"Fine by me," McAllister told him. "I'll be there, same time, same station."

They said their goodbyes and McAllister went back to watching football. But he already knew he'd be telling Simpson about the new jewelry Lemming was wearing. The question that was plaguing him at the moment was whether it would be appropriate to tell Simpson what he saw going on in Smythe's office the week before the jewelry showed up on Lemming's ears and wrist.

He decided to sleep on that. There was no need to make that decision before Tuesday. He went back to his football games, and after a while Julia joined him. The conversation turned to his talk with Simpson, but McAllister told his wife that, when he met Simpson on Tuesday, he had no idea how deep he would go into what he saw at the office. In a moment of reflection, McAllister realized that he was uncommonly concerned with what he should tell Simpson, and that surprised him.

He watched football until the afternoon games were over, but didn't stay up to watch the late games. On occasion he would, but more often than not he used Sunday nights to prepare for work in the morning. There wasn't much preparation necessary for the following day so he found a movie, watching it with Julia until ten o'clock, and then turning in for what turned out to be a fitful night's sleep.

In the morning he still was wondering what to do, how far to go, and what the repercussions could be. He had a day to come to a decision, but the day at work dragged on so slowly that McAllister found himself repeatedly looking at the clock, and finding with a sense of shock that it was only a few minutes later than it was the last time he looked.

Smythe was nowhere to be seen all morning and Lemming made herself scarce too. McAllister was happy with that turn of

The Hypocrite

events, as he had no desire to encounter, much less have a discussion with either of them. Julia packed a lunch for him that morning, so at noon he took it down to the flood control levee overlooking the Connecticut River. He was so preoccupied that he barely tasted the food, although he was vaguely aware that it was excellent. He also took a subconscious note of the river being all but deserted.

The ferryboat stopped running at the end of October and the summer's pleasure boaters were long gone. It didn't matter though. McAllister was just as happy that there was nothing to distract him. He had a big decision to make, and in exactly twenty-four hours it would be over. Until then, he turned the situation over in his mind, again and again, examining it from every angle, looking for the benefits and drawbacks of the options open to him.

Either way someone got what they deserved while someone else got hurt. The questions that were consuming McAllister centered on how much he detested Lemming and Smythe, and how far he was willing to go to get his revenge for the hell they put him and his co-workers through literally from the moment he went to work at Smythe Partners.

In the end, he knew, he had to decide whether to once again out-Christian the Christians—or in this case the faux-Christians, as he had come to call Smythe and Lemming—or just go for the throat, the consequences be damned.

McAllister finished his lunch, enjoyed his routine of listening to oldies music, and prepared for the return to work. He didn't reach a final decision, but at least he was working through his options.

But once again, as he drove back toward Old Main Street, McAllister realized that two cars back from his truck, a black Lexus was trailing him, and once again it had a blue and white sticker on the visor. McAllister might not have noticed it, considering he was

The Hypocrite

preoccupied, but unlike other times when the Lexus was behind him, the cars in between them both turned off at the same spot and the Lexus ended up right on his bumper.

Deciding to get a better look, McAllister suddenly pulled to the side of the street in the middle of a block, stopping quickly and forcing the Lexus to pass him. He looked straight at the driver as the Lexus sped up to pass by McAllister's truck, but didn't recognize the man—noting only that he appeared to be of average stature with thinning hair and spectacles.

The Lexus sped off, heading toward the Silas Deane, and McAllister decided to return to work rather than following it. He spent the afternoon pretty much the same way he spent the morning, deciding to leave an hour early. Lemming wasn't at her desk when he left, Smythe never appeared that day, and he decided to just work through a future lunch hour to make up for the time he took off.

When McAllister pulled into his driveway the sun was still well above the horizon, although it was fading quickly, so he did an extra long workout before dinner. He started with a long run on nearby country roads, returning home only when the sun went down and the gloom of night made it difficult to see. He ran past long stretches of pasture, followed by equally long stretches of dense woodlots.

McAllister's favorite route was four-miles in length and he could run it in multiple variations depending on how far he wanted to go. He also could do it in reverse if he was in the mood for a good challenge, starting out with a relatively flat course that eventually went down a long hill, meaning he would have to come up an equally long hill on the final section.

He had plenty on his mind, so he ran the reverse course, giving him more than three miles of either flats or the downhill stretch to mull over the issues on his mind. The uphill leg would require him to

The Hypocrite

focus on his running at the end, which would make for a good transition into the rest of his workout.

He gave a lot of thought to the issues inside the office as he glided along, but today he also was focused on the black Lexus and why it kept turning up behind him when he ate lunch. It looked remarkably like Smythe's but he realized he never took note of Smythe's license plate number so he couldn't be sure. He did know, however, that each time the Lexus appeared behind him, Smythe's car was not in the office lot when McAllister returned from lunch.

The intensity of his workout released a large dose of endorphins—the body's natural defense against pain—into his system and by the time he was mid-way through his run he was feeling far less stress. When he reached the uphill leg, McAllister put the office out of his mind and concentrated on giving it his all, breaking into a deep sweat as he rounded the corner for home.

He followed the run by lifting weights for nearly an hour. When he finished the final repetitions on the final set of bicep curls, McAllister was sure of the course of action he would take the next day, and from that point on the weight on his shoulders felt much lighter. But just to be sure he had enough time to mull it over, he turned to the heavy punching/kicking bag suspended from the ceiling in the corner of the basement, and began a series of karate kicks and punches. Slow and deliberate at first, then faster, harder, in pre-planned combinations that continued the direction and momentum of the first blow into a series of devastating follow-up shots.

He used turning kicks, hitting with both the instep and bottom of the kicking foot, side snap kicks, crescent kicks and the old mainstay, front snap kicks that every street fighter used for a shot to the family jewels. In between he used his hands—punches, knife-edge strikes, double punches, and finger tip shots to a simulated throat,

The Hypocrite

nose or eyeball target.

McAllister occasionally changed to boxing tactics, using a vicious right hook to the area that would be an opponent's lower ribs, followed quickly by an equally vicious hook to the back of the ear or the temple, incapacitating an opponent on the second shot before the full impact of the first hit to the ribs was felt. Finally, spent and soaked in sweat he slowed down, reducing the power of his hits as well as the speed and frequency, gradually cooling down as he completed the session.

McAllister had told Julia he would cook dinner, and he renewed his promise as he passed her on the way to the shower.

"Are you okay?" Julia asked with more than a little concern in her voice.

"I'm fine, why?"

"You shook the whole house with some of the hits to the bag. It had me worried."

"The whole house?" he asked.

"The whole house," she said again.

"Good," McAllister concluded and headed upstairs.

After showering and dumping his sweats in the washing machine he proceeded to assemble his special version of hamburgers, made with a recipe he inherited from his mother. After cooking them medium-well he placed them on toasted sesame buns, supplementing them with a basic tossed salad and garlic mashed potatoes. Monday night football held out some promise, but at half-time he turned off the television and went to bed.

Once he made his decision, McAllister was anxious for the opportunity to be done with it. He fell asleep almost immediately and didn't wake until he heard Julia moving around the bedroom shortly before 7 a.m. He arose with a sense of anticipation, rather than dread, and was ready for work in near-record time. He even took his time over coffee, reading three full articles in the local morning paper, rather than just scanning the headlines.

He left at his usual time, kissing Julia, but saying nothing about his decision. She walked to the front door, asking only, "Are you okay?" before he stepped outside.

"I'm fine," McAllister answered, and then, noticing her upraised eyebrow—just one, not both—continued, "I'll give you the full rundown when I get home tonight."

McAllister could see that Julia was disappointed, but he learned in the Marines that it usually is best to keep command decisions to oneself until they absolutely have to be revealed. That isn't always the most popular option, but McAllister believed firmly in the adage, "don't telegraph your punches," and that worked equally well in the corporate world or a street fight.

He drove to work, parked, and walked inside, finding Lemming at her desk where she promptly turned away from him and made herself busy with something else. McAllister made no effort at pleasantries, instead simply ascending the staircase and entering his office. Smythe's door was closed and no sound emanated from his office, but as McAllister knew from hard experience, that didn't mean anything.

He fired up the computer, and noted that once again his files were moved or deleted after he left work the previous evening. Without a word he took the backup flash drive from his pocket, restored everything in a matter of minutes and got to work. There was no point in confronting Lemming, but he hoped that someday, somehow, he would get his revenge for her pointless interference.

The Jamieson account was long ago finished, except for some occasional updates, and his work this morning would be the culmination of a proposal for another new client. McAllister was certain it

The Hypocrite

would be accepted, but that didn't mean he took it for granted. He focused all his attention on the project and the morning flew by.

He was actually shocked to look up at the clock and see only ten minutes left before lunch. He wrapped up his work on that phase of the project, and, the destruction of his files still very much on his mind, took the extra step of copying his work to his backup flash drive and taking it with him even though it was only noon.

McAllister drove to Wethersfield with a growing sense of anticipation, pulled into the cemetery and parked in his usual spot. It was sunny, but cold, and he backed the truck up a bit so the branches of the oak tree wouldn't block the sun's warmth from the interior of the cab. He opened his lunch bag to see what Julia had packed for him, taking out a pear and a bottle of fruit juice, when a movement to the side of his truck caught his attention. He was surprised to see Simpson approaching from only a few feet away.

McAllister rolled down his window and greeted Simpson with "You're early today!"

"I'm a bit impatient, I guess," Simpson replied. "Can I impose on you to walk with me today before you start your lunch?"

"Of course," McAllister answered. He closed the brown bag containing the rest of his lunch and placed it on the seat before exiting and joining Simpson.

They walked for several yards in the general direction of Simpson's late wife's grave without saying anything. Simpson suddenly broke the silence. "Did you find out anything or remember anything that could be of help to us?"

"Try as I might I don't remember anyone being in the office all summer, at least since the July meeting, who could have fit the description of a lawyer for the church, as opposed to someone representing one of Moran's clients. In fact, I don't remember anyone be-

The Hypocrite

ing there who wasn't introduced to me. Smythe likes to refer to me as 'the help' and he does it virtually every time someone new comes in.

"But I do have something for you to chew on. I can't prove anything one way or another but a week ago Gail Lemming came to work sporting a new pair of gold earrings with inlaid diamonds, and a gold wrist watch. Neither looked like cheap knockoffs either. From my vantage point they looked like the real deal. And she wasn't the least bit shy about saying she got them from a mysterious benefactor.

"One thing I'm fairly certain about is that she couldn't have afforded them on what I presume would be her salary—based on what skilled labor earns at Smythe Partners."

Simpson walked on in silence, mulling over McAllister's information, finally observing, "That's pretty interesting about the lawyer. Smythe told me several times that he had meetings with our legal counsel right there in the office. Did you take much time off this summer?"

"I'm not eligible for vacation time yet, and I've only had two sick days, when I got a stomach bug, but that was just a couple of weeks ago. In fact, it was when I came back to work in mid-week that Lemming was flashing her new jewelry."

"Why would Smythe give jewelry to Lemming? If, indeed, he was the one who gave it to her?" Simpson asked.

"I don't know the answer to either part of that question," McAllister responded. "I don't know for sure that he gave it to her." He paused then for perhaps a half-minute before adding, "If he did, I don't know why he would."

Simpson turned to him and looked at McAllister for what seemed like a very long minute. But he said nothing and kept walking toward his wife's grave.

That was it, then. McAllister knew exactly who gave the jew-

The Hypocrite

elry to Lemming, at least under the rules of circumstantial evidence, and he sure as hell knew why. But he decided during his workout the previous night that if he told everything he knew to Simpson, there would certainly be collateral damage, most particularly to The Wife.

He didn't know her any better after working for seven months at Smythe Partners, but that didn't mean he had to destroy her life just to get back at Smythe. McAllister was more than familiar with the concept of collateral damage after the fighting he saw in Iraq.

He still carried a hefty sense of frustration with the way the men who fought on the ground were held to a far higher and much more difficult standard than those who fired artillery shells, or bombed from the air. A "grunt," as the infantrymen were called, could do his best in city fighting to clear a building, room by room, doing all in his power to avoid harming civilians without putting himself or his fellow Marines in unnecessary danger.

But the terrorists they were fighting often used civilians as shields, and not just in the classic sense. At times they would run inside a home with Marines or soldiers in hot pursuit, herd the family into a back room, and summarily kill them all.

They would then wait to hear the front door open as the infantry entered, make noise in the back room, and escape out the back door while a grenade was tossed in from the front. When an investigation revealed dead civilians, but no terrorists, it was clear that careers would be ending, and people who were doing the bidding of their government were headed for years in jail.

But if an airplane pilot released a bomb a split second too early or too late, or if an artillery or mortar shell fell in the wrong place, it was written off as the fog of war. It was grossly unfair to the ground pounders, and McAllister hated the hypocrisy behind it. He would not willingly take part in an incident of collateral damage, even back

The Hypocrite

here at home, if he could avoid it. So he told Simpson enough for Simpson to act, but not so much that others would be needlessly drawn into the quagmire that Moran Smythe had made of his life.

Simpson slowed his pace then came to a halt before a relatively new gravestone that bore the name Barbara Simpson. McAllister noted that she died five years earlier at the age of fifty-five.

"She was young," he said to Simpson, more in the manner of an inquiry rather than a question.

"Cancer," Simpson replied. "One day she was the picture of health, but when she came back from her annual physical she told me the doctor said she had untreatable, inoperable bone cancer. We tried everything we could, but her condition deteriorated so fast, that she literally was gone before I even had time to absorb the fact that she was so sick. In the end, all I could do was keep her as comfortable as possible.

"She was the only love of my life," Simpson said, his voice reflecting an enormous sadness, his eyes focused somewhere else, very far away and long ago. "We met in high school, stayed in touch through college and married the year after she graduated. She was a year younger than me, so I had to wait for her graduation. She was the only woman in my life and I was the only man in her life. I never wanted anyone else."

"God, Derrick, I honestly don't know how you got through something like that," McAllister said in total sincerity. "I don't think I could have survived what you went through."

Simpson turned and looked directly at McAllister. "My faith helped me through it. Some people misunderstand what a man like me believes and why. I don't get my thrills by quoting Bible verses that may or may not be what was originally written, or reflective of the original intent.

The Hypocrite

"I have very strong beliefs about my place on this earth and what is waiting for me in the Hereafter. And I don't just say these things, I believe these things. And my beliefs are based almost completely on my own reasoning and observations, not what someone else tells me. Every day when I wake up and look at the world around me I see the beauty we have been given, and I see the ugliness that we have to endure, and sometimes overcome.

"Life is a struggle and sometimes things happen that others say aren't right, or aren't fair. But I see the heights and depths of our mortal life as a natural and normal part of life here on planet earth, and I don't think that just because I am faithful, I am immune from the harsh times.

"I believe with all my heart that I will be with her again. Perhaps in another form, because I also believe the soul lives on after the flesh dies. And I can tell you this without hesitation. If I can go through eternity once again feeling her love, and compassion and tenderness without the pain of our mortal existence, then I believe I will have found the true meaning of Heaven."

They were headed back toward McAllister's truck by now, and McAllister could do nothing but nod, in sympathy and in agreement.

"I know that some people define being devout as going to their place of worship regularly, or being able to quote scripture and tell other people how to live their lives. And I also know that evangelism isn't about just living a good life and making a good example. It's about actively spreading the word of Jesus and the gospel. And I am well aware," he said, again looking directly at McAllister, "that some of the things that are written in the modern versions of the scriptures are not in agreement with the original documents from millennia ago.

"But I believe it is my responsibility here on earth to spread

The Hypocrite

the message, not only in terms of what is written, but also in terms of what I have experienced. And one of the reasons we have regular prayer and Bible study meetings is to talk about, hash out, and sometimes even debate what those original scriptures said or meant and how they relate to us today."

They walked on, again in silence, and finally Simpson looked over at McAllister once again. "I was waiting for your snappy comeback. I figured you'd have a response to all of this."

"As the saying goes 'sometimes less is more,' and I believe this is one of those times," McAllister answered quietly.

"Okay. But no questions or observations?"

"Actually, I do have one question," McAllister said, "and I mean no disrespect. But I noticed your wife died five years ago. Do you ever think about remarrying? Do you have any interest there at all?"

"I don't take offense at your question," Simpson replied. "I get more than my share of inquiries. In the matter of companionship, I have some great friends both in and out of my congregation, and they are very good about including me in group events. It was a bit awkward at first because some thought I'd feel like a third wheel, but when they found that I was comfortable in my own skin and my own circumstances, things got easier.

"There also have been more than a few women who have let me know they are interested and available, some quietly, some overtly, perhaps even blatantly. But Barbara was the one woman for me, and while I know that if I was lonely or needed someone else, she would be the first one to say 'go for it,' the spirit just hasn't moved me in that direction.

"And, if I develop an overwhelming need for a good debate or trustworthy ally, I always have you!" McAllister couldn't help laughing out loud at that one, even as he realized that what Simpson just

The Hypocrite

said was only partly in jest.

By now they were back at the truck and Simpson made ready to leave. "I appreciate your candor, your thoroughness and especially the fact that you didn't jump to unwarranted conclusions. I know the past few months have not been easy for you and no one would blame you for wanting to see Smythe and Lemming get their just desserts," he said. "I'll let you get back to your lunch," Simpson said, turning abruptly and starting for the cemetery entrance.

"Before you go, have you come to any conclusions?" McAllister asked.

Simpson paused. "Yes, I have. I think that even though we probably can't prove it, we both know how Lemming got that jewelry. Perhaps we'll never know why and I don't even want to engage in speculation there. As far as a lawyer is concerned, we're pretty confident there isn't one. If there is, then Smythe should have no problem producing receipts for his time or work. If not, then we're going to the authorities."

McAllister took a minute to absorb Simpson's comments, then asked, "Do you mind if I make a suggestion?"

When Simpson shook his head in the negative, McAllister said, "Why don't you hold off until after Thanksgiving? It's only two days away and nothing will change between now and next week. But at least everyone can enjoy the day, before things get ugly."

"Good advice," Simpson responded. "I'll let the elders know that we'll meet next week and settle this. Enjoy your Thanksgiving."

McAllister responded in kind and Simpson headed for the entrance. McAllister climbed into the truck cab and checked the digital clock. He still had time to eat without hurrying, and he opened the brown bag again to see what Julia had in store for him.

What he found was an especially pleasant surprise. Julia made

The Hypocrite

her "world-famous" crab meat salad on an English muffin for his lunch. She also packed a combination of tomatoes and cucumber slices in a plastic container, as well as the Bartlett pear and juice he removed from the bag just before Simpson appeared. They were sitting in the cup holders on the console, out of the sun and still cool to the touch.

But as McAllister soon discovered, when he left to go with Simpson he put the lunch bag containing his sandwich back on the seat in the sun and for at least twenty minutes it was beaming down directly on the bag containing the crab meat sandwich. As McAllister bit into it he discovered that not only was the crab meat nicely warmed, but the slice of cheese Julia placed over it was partially melted too. It was beyond delicious and he made a mental note to let Julia know just how much he appreciated her efforts for him.

The impact of Simpson's talk was not lost on him. His recent life was unsure, strange even. Not just the part at The Zoo, but before then, too, starting with the attacks of 9-11 and continuing on through his time in the Marines, especially in the war.

There was so much about life on earth that was wonderful, beautiful even, and it could be lost so quickly, with virtually no warning and no reason that the average person could discern. McAllister realized that he often went through life so focused on his immediate concerns that he lost track of the larger picture and the good things that were all around him.

He decided, as he prepared for the drive back to the office, that it might be a good idea to take some time over the holiday to get his priorities in order—as in worrying a lot less about those aspects of life that were out of his control and paying a lot more attention to those things where he actually had some input.

But as McAllister pulled out of the cemetery driveway, he

The Hypocrite

caught a glimpse of something familiar, a blue and white sticker on the visor of a dark sedan, parked directly across the street in the lot behind the Center Tavern facing him. McAllister cut the wheel hard, halting his turn to the right that would have brought him to the stop sign at the intersection, instead shooting straight across to the tavern parking lot and heading straight for the Lexus.

The car was driven by the same man who was in it the day before, and McAllister jumped from the cab of the Ford to confront him. But the driver had the car running, intending to follow McAllister when he took his usual route back to work. The driver now was wearing a shocked and frightened look on his face.

He threw the Lexus into drive and hit the accelerator, firing out of the parking spot and shooting loose dirt and gravel behind him. Some of it hit McAllister, but he ignored it and instead memorized the license plate. It wasn't hard. The plate said SMYTHE1, and McAllister knew exactly where that car usually was parked.

He returned to his truck and drove back to the office at a leisurely pace, but as he pulled into the drive, a small pickup truck blasted past him going the other way. It occurred to McAllister that he had seen that truck parked in the office lot many times previously, and he figured it belonged to one of the workers in the back office.

But the driver today was the same man he saw the previous day and just a few minutes ago in Wethersfield. The truck wasted no time getting away from the Smythe Partners property, and again McAllister decided against following it. Because today, parked in the spot reserved for the owner of Smythe Partners, was a black Lexus bearing the license plate SMYTHE1, and upon further inspection, McAllister confirmed that it had a blue and white sticker—for the town park as it turned out—on the visor.

McAllister cracked the knuckles of his fists and smiled grimly

The Hypocrite

as he strode to the door. Inside Lemming was sitting at her desk with her hands folded like an urchin.

"Is Moran upstairs?" McAllister queried as he headed for the staircase.

"He's not in," Lemming answered with the sticky sweet tone that made McAllister want to throw her off the roof.

"His car is in the lot, so where is he?" McAllister demanded.

"Just because his car is here, doesn't mean he is here. And if he wanted you to know where he is, he would have told you."

McAllister knew a dead end when he saw one and terminated the conversation. Besides, this could wait. Smythe would have to come out of hiding sooner or later and when he did, McAllister would be there.

Chapter 12

The Road to Hell

Bruce McAllister actually had a bit of a spring in his step as he walked toward the front door of Smythe Partners, Ltd., on the Monday morning after Thanksgiving.

The holiday break did wonders for his energy levels, especially since Smythe surprised the entire office, including Lemming, by not showing up for work the previous Wednesday and then calling Lemming to tell her he was letting everyone go home at noon—with pay! When McAllister walked in the front door of his home at midday, Julia was very happy to see him. But when she inquired how he managed to come home early, he responded that Smythe was "trying to get in good with God."

Whatever the reason for Smythe's generosity—and McAllister had a very good idea of its source—it gave him and Julia some added time together. She was getting ready to go shopping for Thanksgiving dinner, so McAllister accompanied her, picking up the fresh, organically raised turkey they had ordered a few weeks earlier, and selecting the ingredients for his mushroom and sausage stuffing while she got the vegetables.

The Hypocrite

On the way home they stopped at a local farm stand to pick up their pre-ordered raspberry pie. It was a frozen pie that probably wouldn't set well with purists who preferred to bake their pies the night before Thanksgiving, but Julia discovered in previous years that this farm's frozen pies were the equivalent of those prepared fresh by many of her friends.

Their shopping trip set the stage for a weekend of togetherness, without the stress of the daily antics at Smythe Partners, and for a time they were able to put work way in the background and just enjoy themselves.

That in turn resulted in McAllister's upbeat mood on Monday morning. It was a cold, clear day, the last day of the month and winter was obviously just around the corner. While Monday was to remain cold, the forecast for the next three days was for unseasonable warmth, but a return to cold weather and a possible snowstorm was forecast for the end of the week.

McAllister was dressed for the cold, wearing the overcoat that had hung on a hanger deep in his closet since the previous spring. He opened the door, stepped into the reception area and immediately was confronted by Smythe and Lemming. Neither seemed to be in a good mood, and both glared at him as he entered the building.

Before he could speak, Smythe spoke up, "Don't bother taking that coat off McAllister. You're not going to spend this day in the office!"

McAllister was momentarily surprised but had the presence of mind to ask, "What's going on Moran?"

Lemming smirked, which was never a good sign, but Smythe replied only that, "I have a client appointment in Southington in an hour and you're going with me. You don't need anything from your office so head back out to the car and I'll be out as soon as I'm fin-

The Hypocrite

ished here."

McAllister turned on his heel and walked back to the parking lot. "Talk about a buzz kill," McAllister said to himself as he walked outside. "That didn't take long."

He looked for Smythe's Lexus but it wasn't in its usual spot. What was there instead was a new Range Rover, a large top-of-the-line vehicle that McAllister had not seen before. It was black, and as McAllister looked inside the tinted windows, he saw what appeared to be an all black interior with walnut colored finishes and leather airline type seats. It was a great looking vehicle.

"Fifty-K wouldn't even buy the wheels for that baby!" Smythe came down the walk behind him and was beaming over his latest possession, which well could have been the reason why McAllister was going on this trip in the first place. The foul mood he appeared to be in a few minutes earlier seemed to dissipate as Smythe took the opportunity to impress a groundling with his new vehicle.

"Get in," he ordered, clicking the button on his key ring to unlock the doors.

McAllister did as ordered and inhaled that "new car smell" which he hadn't experienced in a number of years. The interior could only be described as plush, and Smythe obviously purchased a model that included all the bells and whistles.

They departed Smythe Partners, drove to the Silas Deane Highway and from there to the entrance ramp to I-91 South. Smythe accelerated smoothly up the ramp, but once he got to the highway, he took a quick look over his shoulder and then he punched it. The Rover literally leaped ahead, quickly matching and then easily surpassing the flow of traffic on the highway.

"That's a five-liter engine under the hood," Smythe boasted. "Supercharged," he added.

The Hypocrite

McAllister said a silent prayer that they'd survive the day, a questionable matter considering Smythe's driving habits and the potential speed of the new car. McAllister had read somewhere recently that the Range Rover had advanced safety features and could only hope that they were up to the task of Smythe's recklessness.

The town of Southington is about a half-hour from Rocky Hill, first going south on I-91, then west on the I-691 connector to I-84 and then one exit east on I-84. It is more town than city but still has an active commercial and industrial base, and is known for its good schools and well-run local government.

Considering the destination, there was good reason to anticipate a pleasant trip, and McAllister promised himself that he would do his best to keep quiet, remembering all too well the way Smythe drove on the trip to the Jamieson facility in Union several months earlier. To that end he sat back and enjoyed the memories of the just passed Thanksgiving weekend.

He and Julia decided not to accept any of the several invitations they received from family and friends to go elsewhere for the holiday. Even though they would be dining alone, they agreed that a few days to themselves would be welcome. Besides, they both enjoyed cooking. The Thanksgiving Day menu was one they had developed over several years, and they looked forward to it.

They spent Thanksgiving morning preparing the turkey and stuffing it with his special recipe, and then put it into the oven. Julia ordered a relatively small bird this year, only ten pounds, but there still would be plenty of meat left over for a second dinner, plus turkey sandwiches, turkey ala king and in the end, turkey soup. Some of the leftovers would be eaten in the next couple of days, while the remainder would be frozen as a hedge against the cold winter days that were only a week or so away.

The Hypocrite

The rest of the weekend was spent relaxing. They took a drive on Saturday afternoon, stopping for lunch at a small roadside eatery along the coast, enjoying lobster sandwiches and cold beer. They watched a movie Saturday night and settled in for an afternoon of football on Sunday. Overall it was a fun and relaxing break for both of them.

McAllister found himself smiling as he remembered the past few days but was jolted out of his reveries by a sudden question from Smythe. "So, what was the outcome of your little meeting with Simpson?'

Smythe's tone was cold and McAllister took a few seconds before responding. "What meeting with Simpson?'

"Don't play stupid with me, McAllister. Do you think I don't know about the secret meeting my fellow parishioners had in my absence the Saturday before Thanksgiving? Do you think I don't know that Simpson thinks of you as his little spy? Do you think I don't know about your meeting him in the cemetery at lunch time last Tuesday? Do you honestly think you are smarter and wiser than I am?"

"Moran, I won't even speculate on the level of your intellect," McAllister responded. "And I don't have the slightest idea what goes on in your church, nor do I care. But as far as meeting Simpson in the cemetery is concerned, I have never made a secret of going there for lunch from time to time. I've told you directly. And Mr. Simpson goes there to visit his wife's grave from time to time and occasionally I run into him there. So what!"

"Then why were you at the zoning meeting the Thursday before Thanksgiving week?" Smythe's voice was rising and McAllister noticed his speed was picking up simultaneously.

"Hold on a minute. This is getting confusing. A second ago you

The Hypocrite

were talking about my meeting Simpson at the cemetery the Tuesday before Thanksgiving. Now you're on the zoning meeting the Thursday before that, and there was what, a church meeting on the Saturday in between? I'm having trouble keeping this straight." McAllister was well aware of the time line involved, but he was buying himself some space to formulate his responses to Smythe's inquiries.

"I'm talking about the zoning meeting on Thursday night the week before Thanksgiving. Why did you show up there?" Smythe was speaking between tightly clenched teeth and nearly hissed his words.

"I already told you why I went to that meeting. Simpson told me months ago that the elders in your church were disappointed about my missing their lunch with you in July. He said you told them I might be able to suggest some possible solutions to the problem with getting your building permits for the church. He said you told them that I think outside the box and maybe a fresh set of eyes on the issue would help.

"I told you then, and I'm telling you again, that Gail Lemming never told me about that July meeting until just before noon that day, and she never told me about the purpose. And I told you just a week ago that I felt bad about not making it, and I went to the zoning meeting just before Thanksgiving to see if I could help.

"As far as whatever meeting was held the Saturday after the zoning meeting, I am not a member of your church. I am not involved in either its external or internal affairs, and I wasn't there."

"You might not have been there but you were the subject of some pretty detailed discussions at that Saturday night meeting," Smythe responded. He was well settled into his anger now—a factor that McAllister learned long ago could be used to his advantage if it was kept under control.

The Hypocrite

"I don't know how you are so well versed on what happened at a meeting you didn't attend, and frankly I don't care. But I would certainly like to know why you think I'm Simpson's spy?" McAllister put the ball back in Smythe's court and he ran for it.

"I have my friends in this parish and very little goes on in my absence that I don't know about. And as far as knowing about you and Simpson at the cemetery, you were seen there."

"By you or someone else?" McAllister demanded. He knew that tone of voice would keep Smythe at an appropriate level of anger, which meant he wouldn't be thinking straight and would divulge more information than he might if he were more in control of himself.

"And by the way, while we're on the subject, who was that pissant you had following me in your Lexus? I want to speak with him, one on one. Where is the Lexus?"

"None of your damned business," Smythe replied, again with teeth clenched so tight McAllister was surprised they didn't burst under the stress. Smythe was nearly to the roaring stage now and coming dangerously close to being out of control.

However, McAllister wanted more information than he had at the moment and decided to push the envelope just a bit further. "So you are having someone else spy on me. And you accuse me of being a spy? That's rich."

"I don't stalk people!" Smythe yelled. "And I still want to know how you found out about the zoning meeting, if it wasn't from Simpson."

"I already told you, I heard Lemming on the phone talking about it," McAllister replied tersely.

"I asked Gail about that and she denied it!" Smythe again was hollering.

The Hypocrite

"Well, you might want to rethink what you tell her," McAllister responded. "Every time you leave the office she makes a point of letting everyone know how much she has the inside track. She just can't wait to tell us what a big noise she is in Smythe Partners."

McAllister wasn't lying to Smythe when he said he heard about the zoning meeting from Lemming. She really was talking about it on the phone, and the fact that he also heard about it from Simpson was redundant. So he didn't go into that.

And he didn't relate to Smythe that Simpson called him at home again the previous day, the same as he did the weekend before Thanksgiving. The call came at halftime in the Sunday afternoon football game, the same as the weekend before, and Simpson was sparse in the information he gave to McAllister.

He said only that he was calling another meeting for Thursday night and that Smythe would be told about it and given the opportunity to bring Lemming as well. Simpson told McAllister, "I didn't tell anyone about the jewelry Lemming is wearing, not even the most trusted elders in the church. I figure that can come up at a more appropriate time."

McAllister already knew that Simpson was a smart guy, but as the situation with Smythe unfolded he was impressed anew each time another development arose. Thinking about their conversation later on Sunday afternoon, McAllister realized that the less Simpson revealed of what he knew about the internal issues in Smythe Partners, the more McAllister was protected from retaliation.

He also knew that when he got home that night he would call Simpson and alert him that he had a mole in his organization. Someone who was at the Saturday night meeting the weekend before Thanksgiving obviously gave Smythe a blow-by-blow report. That person gave Smythe far more information on what transpired there

The Hypocrite

than McAllister possessed. McAllister didn't even know what was meant by spying for Simpson, unless it was the questions Simpson asked him at their meeting in the cemetery a week ago.

But even that was pretty mild. Did he ever see a lawyer who was representing the church come to Smythe's office, and did he see any evidence of unusual expenditures? No one identified as a church lawyer came to the office all summer, and the jewelry Lemming was wearing was an obvious departure from the norm. But it was nowhere near as expensive as the vehicle in which they were now riding. McAllister realized he wouldn't have to say anything about the Range Rover—it pretty much spoke for itself.

Several minutes passed during which neither man spoke until Smythe suddenly shouted, "Well?"

"Well what?" McAllister asked.

"Well, is that all you have to say? Why aren't you answering me?"

"I did answer you, Moran. Maybe you weren't listening or didn't like what I had to say, but I did answer. And I haven't said anything else because I was thinking about the client we're going to see, and what I might say to help us get a new account. What did you say they do—some kind of new age marketing?"

"Something like that," Smythe growled. "Gail Lemming has been doing some research for me. She's helping me look for potential clients. This economy isn't getting any better and we need to keep up our efforts. We'll find out when we get there."

McAllister refrained from making any comments about proper preparation for client meetings, or for that matter about the wisdom of having Lemming do anything that was more complicated than answering a phone. He returned to his previous silence, looking out the passenger window at the barren Connecticut landscape. During

The Hypocrite

their exchange Smythe drove from I-91 to I-691 and now was on the entrance ramp to I-84 eastbound. Within minutes they were on West Main Street in Southington and pulling into the parking lot at the prospective client's address.

They exited the vehicle in silence, but this time Smythe refrained from telling McAllister that he couldn't talk during the interview. They walked to the front door, and entered the lobby where, as McAllister later described it to Julia, things immediately went from weird to freaky.

The receptionist possibly could have been an attractive young woman, but it was nearly impossible to tell for sure. She was wearing a sleeveless blouse, low cut, revealing tattoos, lots of tattoos, that didn't really capture McAllister's attention because she also had a head full of multi-colored hair. Her "do" included many hues that are not in the rainbow, and a face full of what he called "stuff," but what others would call piercings.

She had literally dozens of piercings in her ears, nose, eyelids, forehead, her face, lips and even two on her tongue. McAllister refrained from mentally considering where else she might be pierced, as the image could not possibly be attractive.

The woman looked at them as if they had just exited a space ship, asking, "Can I help you?"

Smythe introduced himself and said they had an appointment with the plant manager.

"We don't use that term here," the receptionist told Smythe. "We prefer the term facilitator."

"I'll remember that," Smythe replied dryly.

The receptionist spoke into her headset and said to Smythe, "He'll be right with you."

There was nothing in the lobby that even hinted at what the

The Hypocrite

company did, and McAllister was at a loss as to what he could offer to help secure a new contract. He needn't have worried. In less than a minute, a door to the left of the receptionist's desk opened and a male, appearing to be in his late twenties, who could have been her twin, at least in terms of his decorations, entered the room. His hair was spiked, and it too, was multi-colored, and his clothing was—unusual.

The 'facilitator' stopped a few steps outside the door, looked first at Smythe, then at McAllister. "Is one of you Smythe?" he asked without introducing himself.

"I am," Smythe responded. "Moran Smythe."

The man looked at them for a few more seconds then said, "I'm sorry gentlemen. This won't do. I'm not going to bother with the interview. I can see already that you're not a good fit for this company."

He turned to leave but Smythe literally exploded. "What the hell do you mean by that? How can you tell anything just by looking at us? We just drove the better part of an hour to sit down with you and you just tell us to turn around and leave?"

Smythe was obviously angry, frustrated and totally confused. McAllister had never heard him swear before, but looking at the facilitator he knew they were definitely in the wrong place.

"First off, I did a reverse locator map check on your company and it is only thirty-five minutes from your office to ours. But that isn't the issue. Look at yourself, man," the facilitator said, responding to Smythe. "You're button down, dude. And so is your associate. Do you see anything about this place that looks button-down? No you don't, and you won't.

"I'm not looking for button-down traditional vendors. I'm looking for outside-the-box. I want freaks whose minds go down uncharted paths. You do not fit the bill and I'm not going to waste your

The Hypocrite

time or mine. There's the door."

Smythe was nonplussed, seemingly in a daze, and walked out to the sidewalk, with McAllister a few steps behind, doing everything in his power not to laugh out loud. He wasn't happy at all about losing a potential client, but he simply had never seen such an odd company in an industrial park, nor had he ever seen anyone dismiss Smythe so offhandedly. All in all it was quite a show.

They reentered the Range Rover and Smythe slammed his door with all his might. Fortunately, McAllister's door was still partially open and he didn't suffer any noticeable damage to his ear drums. Smythe pulled out his cell phone, hit a number on speed dial and in a few seconds was talking to Lemming.

"What the hell did you do?" he shouted at her. "Where did you send us? This place is a circus! How did you ever line up a meeting like this? I want to see you in my office the instant we get back!"

If he could have slammed the phone down, he would have. Smythe satisfied his violent urges by tossing the phone into the cup holder on the console before starting the Rover and racing the engine.

Smythe backed out of the parking space, squealing his tires in the process and blasted down the drive toward West Main Street. Fortunately, at least regarding the local police department, the client's office wasn't that far from the highway and Smythe was on the entrance ramp before anyone could report his erratic driving.

If McAllister was concerned at Smythe's speeding previously, he was about to experience an entirely new world of adrenaline-induced sensations. Smythe stomped the gas pedal to the floor and didn't let up until they were already on the exit ramp for I-691 heading back toward I-91. The ramp turned tightly to the left, crossing I-84 before it straightened out, and Smythe severely tested the Range

The Hypocrite

Rover's stability, in addition to the laws of physics, as they related to the vehicle's center of gravity. But even the sharpness of the entrance ramp curve didn't seem to calm Smythe's rage or temper his driving.

As soon as the road straightened out, Smythe again stomped the accelerator to the floor. He was over 100 m.p.h. in a matter of seconds and seemed hell-bent on finding the vehicle's top speed. Unlike the previous trip to Union, where Smythe could easily have killed them both if he hadn't been caught in a police speed trap, McAllister was not about to sit quietly this time.

"How about you calm down and get back in the neighborhood of the speed limit," he told Smythe in a cold, but calm voice.

"What's the matter, Marine? Are you scared, Marine? I thought big, tough Marines aren't scared of anything!" Smythe was taunting McAllister, saying the word Marine with a sneer. "I've got eight forward gears in this transmission and we're going to try them all out before I get to I-91. What do you think of that, Marine?"

"I think I've got a better idea. You pull this vehicle over right now, let me out and I'll thumb a ride back to the office. Do it now Smythe!"

Smythe didn't even respond. He was coming up on slower vehicles at an incredible speed, weaving in and out of traffic like a madman. Smythe was looking at McAllister when he was told to pull over and nearly crashed into the rear of a Ford SUV in front of him.

Smythe looked forward and yanked the wheel to the left just in time to avoid crashing into the bumper of the other car, swerving into the fast lane and just as quickly, apparently to display the level of his anger and ignorance at the same time, swerved back in front of the car he had just passed, this time nearly clipping the front bumper.

The near accident really ticked off the driver in the Ford, who as it turned out, was just about as stupid as Smythe and just as likely to

The Hypocrite

erupt into fits of rage on the highway. He, in turn, floored his vehicle and quickly caught up to Smythe, who had slowed just a bit after realizing he nearly crashed his new Range Rover. The second driver continued the dispute by first tailgating Smythe—as in maybe two feet off the Rover's bumper—then passing Smythe and cutting him off as Smythe had to him only a moment earlier.

Smythe, typically, then began tailgating the Ford, and the driver of that vehicle did a "brake check" locking up his brakes, smoking his tires, leaving about five thousand miles of rubber on the road in the form of skid marks. This further infuriated Smythe, if that was even possible, who in turn passed the Ford so he could do the same thing to the other driver.

Both SUVs were travelling in the neighborhood of 120 miles per hour and flew over the hill that separates the communities of Cheshire and Southington from the city of Meriden. They flew down the hill, forcing other drivers out of the way and quickly hit the section in Meriden where I-691 spreads out to at least three lanes, four in some places where there were lengthy exit ramps.

It gave both idiots plenty of room to maneuver and they did. The fact that either one could have called the whole thing off, simply by slowing down or taking an exit, obviously didn't occur to them. They weaved in and out of the traffic that fortunately was very sparse at this hour of the morning, still blasting along at three-digit speeds.

They passed over Connecticut Rt. 15 and were fast approaching the left exit that Smythe would have to take to enter I-91 north. The highway was back to two lanes but the Ford driver used the right hand breakdown lane to pass a slower vehicle—that driver had the good sense to pull over and stop his vehicle. He immediately called 911 to report the road rage incident he was watching play out in front of him—and his passenger took cell phone pictures of both

The Hypocrite

vehicles including the license plates.

The Ford driver was back in the slow lane now, but there were no other cars on that stretch of highway. Smythe, stupidly thinking the incident was over, didn't look to his right rear, didn't see the Ford in his blind spot, and began slowing to make the exit. But the Ford sped ahead of him and once again the driver did a quick lane switch, intending to force Smythe to slam on his brakes. But it didn't work that way.

The rear bumper of the Ford caught the passenger side edge of the Rover's front bumper and the Rover went into what McAllister saw as a slow-motion spin to the left. At that speed, it hit the guardrail in a millisecond, and McAllister watched in horror as the bumper and the hood both flew off, up into the air, landing behind them somewhere as the air bags deployed, the passenger side bag hitting him solidly in the face. McAllister had a split second to think that his life was about to end and an incredible sense of sadness overcame him as he thought of Julia and all their plans that would never come to fruition.

But in one of those weird twists of fate that happen sometimes in traffic accidents, the Rover spun back to the right, ending up going straight, with the Ford several car lengths ahead. The brakes were still working and Smythe was literally standing on them, leaving four long black streaks of smoking rubber behind them.

And then, everything stopped. The Rover stopped, the Ford stopped, and the noise stopped. McAllister couldn't believe that he was still intact, apparently unscathed, except for his face where the air bag hit him.

But Smythe still wouldn't let it go. McAllister watched aghast as Smythe threw open the driver's side door, his face a contorted picture of out-of-control rage. The air bag was now deflated, and McAl-

The Hypocrite

lister could see that the driver of the Ford also had left his vehicle and was striding menacingly back toward the Rover.

Smythe began hollering at the other driver, who in turn began responding to Smythe. It looked as though the two fools would hash out their road rage issues with their fists right there in the breakdown lane, amid the debris.

The other driver was fair skinned, shorter than Smythe, but heavily muscled. He was wearing jeans, work boots and a light jacket that was unzipped revealing a tank top style shirt underneath. His car was not damaged except for the rear bumper and even that was not too bad. It could be fixed easily, McAllister surmised. The driver could have just sped away with no one the wiser. But neither he nor Smythe would back down.

Smythe was still yelling, something about kicking the other man's rear end, but he didn't say rear end. In fact, McAllister heard numerous instances of the F-bomb exploding including several from Smythe, as well as numerous instances of taking the Lord's name in vain, which didn't seem to be in keeping with Smythe's Christian beliefs.

For the first few seconds after the accident was over McAllister figured he'd just let the drivers beat each other senseless and when they were done, figure out how to get back to Rocky Hill. Then, once again, everything changed in an instant.

He saw a flash of light and realized it was the sun reflecting off an object in the Ford driver's right hand—and that object was a pistol! McAllister leaped from the Rover and ran around to the front yelling, "Smythe, back off, man. Smythe!"

Smythe did not, would not, or could not listen. When he was within a dozen feet or so of the other driver the pistol barked. Smythe stopped, turning slightly toward McAllister with a look of shocked

The Hypocrite

disbelief on his face, a bright red smear quickly spreading over his dress shirt. Smythe's legs buckled under him and he slowly sagged to the ground. His last words were the curses he hurled at the Ford driver.

Smythe died there, on the cold ground, in a spreading pool of blood. With him went the better part of four centuries of the Smythe dynasty. It died in the midst of a criminal activity, exactly as it had begun. In the hundreds of years since the first Moran Smythe became a businessman by killing the owner of a long-gone tavern, his descendants had moved barely ten miles from the starting point, and accomplished—nothing.

McAllister looked at the other driver who advanced several more steps. He was looking down at the pistol, then at Smythe, as though he couldn't believe what he had just done. McAllister was less than ten feet from him now, and could see his blue eyes and the frightened quickness of the Ford driver's breathing. He could also see that the pistol was a large caliber model, probably something in the range of a forty-five.

"Put the gun down, man," McAllister ordered. "Put it down. This is over. This didn't have to happen, but it's over. Put the gun down, NOW!"

The man looked at McAllister as if he were seeing him for the first time. "No witnesses. I can't have any witnesses."

For the first time all morning, just when he needed witnesses the most, McAllister realized there was not another car in sight. Traffic on that section of I-691 was often light outside of rush hours, but this was beyond light, this was non-existent.

The gunman looked frightened, and out of control, and now he swung the pistol in McAllister's direction. McAllister didn't look at the pistol, he looked straight into the man's face, watching, and

The Hypocrite

not moving. Suddenly, he saw the gunman's eyes widen and his nostrils flare. McAllister leaped to his right. The gun barked again, and McAllister felt something that he had not felt since he was in Iraq—every single nerve in his body seemed to explode in pain, then went numb.

He looked down but saw no wound, no blood. He hadn't felt the impact of a bullet hitting when the shot was fired, and there was no evidence that he was hit. Then he looked at the gunman. McAllister was vaguely aware that when the pistol fired, he heard two sounds, like metal on metal—twice. Two sounds, not one, two.

The gunman had a look of wonderment on his face, as if he couldn't comprehend all that had just happened. Then a red smear, similar to the one on Smythe's shirt that still was spreading across the road where he lay, began spreading out on the gunman's tank top, and like Smythe, he too sagged to the road, the pistol falling from his hand.

McAllister went to Smythe's side and quickly determined that he was dead. He walked back to the gunman, planning to kick the pistol far enough away so that he couldn't reach it, but realized that the second driver also was dead or very close to it. In what seemed like only a few more seconds, a state police cruiser blasted up to the scene, lights on and siren wailing, screeching to a halt within feet of where McAllister was standing. The trooper jumped out, pistol drawn and pointed straight at McAllister.

In all that had just happened, it was not lost on McAllister that he had two pistols pointed at him within minutes of each other all on the same morning, and he was the only person in the mix who had done nothing wrong.

"Clasp your hands on top of your head," the trooper ordered in a loud voice. "Do it!"

The Hypocrite

McAllister complied immediately.

"Move to the vehicle to your left, face it and place both of your hands on the fender."

McAllister again complied immediately, putting his hands on the passenger side front fender of the Rover, and upon a further order from the trooper spread his feet beyond shoulder width. He said nothing as the trooper first frisked him, and then pulled McAllister's wallet from his right rear trouser pocket. The trooper located McAllister's license and asked if he was Bruce McAllister.

When McAllister replied in the affirmative, the trooper asked, "Well, Mr. McAllister, would you like to tell me what happened here today?"

"Sure," McAllister answered.

"What?" the trooper asked. He wasn't used to people complying that willingly.

"I said 'sure,'" McAllister repeated.

"Okay then, what the hell happened?"

"Basically," McAllister said, "the driver of the Ford and the driver of the Rover got into a road rage situation, which caused this accident, and they both got out, continuing their fight, but the Ford driver had a pistol and he shot the Rover driver and then tried to shoot me but shot himself instead."

The trooper took a few seconds to digest what he had just heard, then asked, "And what was your part in this fiasco?"

McAllister also paused for a few seconds, and then said quietly, "I was either a witness to or a participant in a miracle—or both."

As he finished his comments three more cruisers arrived, literally in unison. A sergeant was quickly alongside the first trooper and took command of the scene. The trooper explained to his superior what he had seen and had been told, and the sergeant ordered him to

The Hypocrite

place McAllister in the rear of the first cruiser until they could sort out the situation.

McAllister was just about to sit in the back seat when the sergeant turned and asked, "Mr. McAllister were you injured in any way during this?"

McAllister told him of the air bags deploying when the Rover hit the guardrail, and after another question from the sergeant, said that he didn't feel injured but wouldn't object to a medical team examining him when they arrived. The next hour was a blur, as McAllister could only see a small part of the action. An officer moved the cruiser where he sat to a position in front of the Ford SUV. He was facing forward, although he could turn to watch the police and medical examiner personnel going about their work.

After a time, five troopers, the sergeant, the first trooper on the scene, a lieutenant and two accident reconstruction specialists, came to the cruiser and allowed McAllister out to stretch his legs. They asked him if he wanted a lawyer but McAllister declined, and then they asked him to describe the events leading up to the shootings.

He did so in detail and answered all their questions, including in his report the two metallic sounds he heard when the gunman fired the second time. They asked him the same questions several times, changing the questions slightly each time, but his story never wavered. It couldn't, he was telling them the truth.

Eventually, two crime scene investigators joined them and asked if he would object to being tested for gunshot residue. McAllister didn't object and they did their test, swabbing his hands and wrists, and asking him to hand over his shirt, which he did. When they were finished the lieutenant ordered them to expedite the preliminary test, which wasn't that hard because the shootout occurred less than fifteen minutes from the state police forensic laboratory.

The Hypocrite

Meanwhile, other specialists were arriving in a steady stream. Over the course of another hour, an expanded team of accident reconstruction and crime scene reconstruction experts repeatedly interviewed McAllister about the sounds he heard after the second gunshot. Finally, about three hours after the gunfire, the police approached McAllister and told him he could exit the cruiser.

"Mr. McAllister, you said that when the shooter fired the second shot, the one aimed at you, that you jumped to your right. Can you explain to us why you did that?"

"Sure," McAllister replied. "I have experience with firearms and people in high intensity situations. I know it is common for a relatively inexperienced person to jerk the trigger when they fire. Generally, a right-handed person will pull to the right and a left-handed person will pull to the left. I figured if he jerked the trigger, the shot would go wide to my left—his right—and if I jumped to the right at the same time he might just miss me."

"How did you know when he would fire," the lieutenant asked.

"I was watching his eyes. He was staring at me like a madman, but just as he pulled the trigger his eyes flared, and so did his nostrils. When I saw that I jumped."

"You said you have experience with firearms and high stress situations," the sergeant said. "Can you explain that a bit more?"

"I served two enlistments in the Marines, and that included three combat tours in Iraq."

"Did you fight?" the sergeant asked.

"I made the initial assault up to Baghdad, and then I went to Fallujah, and elsewhere in Anbar," McAllister answered.

He saw several of the troopers nod their heads in the affirmative.

"Mr. McAllister," the lieutenant said, "we're going to release

The Hypocrite

you on your own recognizance. There is no evidence that you did anything wrong. The preliminary tests on your skin swabs and on your shirt show no gunshot residue. And our crime scene reconstruction people have found what appears to be a bullet mark on the steel spring of the Rover's suspension and a similar mark on the guardrail.

"They say it looks as though the shooter jerked the gun, as you anticipated, and the bullet hit the steel suspension component at the perfect angle to ricochet off toward the guardrail, and then it further ricocheted back into the shooter's midsection. It hit him right in the spleen and he bled out right there on the spot."

The trooper looked at McAllister for a long minute and then observed, "They say that shot is possible, but it's something you won't see once in ten million times. The investigator said that if the temperature had been any warmer the steel on the guardrail would have absorbed the impact more and the bullet wouldn't have ricocheted back at the shooter the way it did. It wouldn't have worked with a hollow point bullet either, and this guy was carrying jacketed rounds. It seems that some pretty complicated circumstances had to occur all at once, and they did.

"I don't know if their statistics are right, but I do know that you are a very fortunate man. Three people were here at the beginning of this incident, and if either one of those two had just walked away, or had driven away, nothing further would have happened. But they didn't and now only you are left. That should tell people something."

McAllister didn't answer, but he did nod his head. The impact of all he had seen and had been told in the past few hours was not lost on him in the least. Later, he'd take some time to think about it.

Another trooper approached then. "Mr. McAllister, I'll be giving you a ride up to Rocky Hill so you can retrieve your vehicle. Will you be okay to drive yourself home?"

The Hypocrite

"I can drive," McAllister answered, greatly relieved to be getting away from the mess around him.

The trooper turned, but before McAllister could join him, four other troopers walked up to him. "Semper Fi, Brother," they said as one. "You'll have some pretty big stories to tell your grandchildren some day," a trooper first-class added.

"Semper Fi," McAllister said, repeating the shortened version of the Marine motto, Semper Fidelis—Always Faithful. It was their way of identifying each other when not in uniform.

"The Lord was with you today, Brother," another one said as they began to disperse.

"I have never been more sure of anything in my life," McAllister answered as he entered the cruiser. This time he sat in the front.

Chapter 13

My Name Is...

The phone rang in the McAllister residence on the Sunday after the shootout on I-691 the previous Monday, exactly as halftime started for the 1 p.m. football game.

But unlike other Sundays, this time it wasn't Derrick Simpson on the line, and McAllister wasn't home to take the call. He and Julia had gone for a walk, enjoying the sunny day after the snowstorm that hit Friday morning.

They opted for a walk in the woods behind their house, and stayed on game trails that already bore the prints of deer, rabbits and what appeared to be at least one coyote. The weather was crisp, but not frigid and they both wore multiple layers of winter clothes to stay warm while allowing them to shed outer garments if they wanted to.

They needed the time outside in the sun. They needed to appreciate life and all it offered and suddenly, Sunday afternoon football games took a back seat to the simple priority of appreciating the outdoors. Although the trails were snowy, the storm on Friday dumped only about four inches total and walking through it wasn't difficult.

The Hypocrite

The past week had been a roller coaster of emotional highs and lows, starting with McAllister's return to Smythe Partner's Ltd., in a police cruiser several hours after the shooting Monday morning. An officer called Smythe's home giving The Wife the news about Smythe at about the same time that McAllister was being transported back to the office.

The Wife in turn called the office, relating what had happened and closing the business for the remainder of the day. But when McAllister returned about twenty minutes later most of the other workers were still outside in the parking lot waiting for him.

As he stepped out of the cruiser and thanked the trooper for the ride, they gathered around McAllister, expressing their relief that he was unharmed and questioning what on earth went wrong during what should have been a simple client meeting. McAllister took the time to fill them in on the details of the morning's events, and the ultimate tragedy of two deaths resulting from stupid driving and out-of-control anger.

Ken Wilson, the marketing director, asked how the meeting went, and McAllister filled him in on the strangeness of it all. "How on earth did we even get a lead like that?" Wilson asked.

"Lemming," was McAllister's one-word reply. "Where is she by the way?"

"She took off as soon as the news came in," Wilson informed him. "She wasn't at her desk when the phone rang so one of the ladies in bookkeeping answered. She called the rest of us together, including Lemming, and told us what happened. Lemming let out some kind of weird wail and then stormed out the door."

"I suppose their final conversation might be behind that," McAllister told him. Then, elaborating on it because Wilson looked puzzled, he said, "Smythe called her the instant we were back in the car

The Hypocrite

and tore into her. He said he wanted to see her upstairs as soon as we got back. I guess that meeting is cancelled." He knew the last comment might be seen as irreverent, but he didn't regret making it, considering the events of the morning.

Wilson pondered McAllister's statements for a few minutes, and then said, "I know this has been a terrible day for you. But do you have a few minutes? There are some things I think you should know."

McAllister said he could stay for a few more minutes, but then wanted to get home to his wife. Wilson asked him to walk toward their vehicles giving them distance from the rest of the staff.

"I have been tossing this around in my mind since last summer," he started out. "I know more about what was going on with Smythe and Lemming than I told you, and I feel bad about it, but I didn't want to lose my job in this economy."

"Go on," was McAllister's only response.

"Well, based on what happened today and the fact that I might never see you again, I figure you should know this. Smythe threw a party last winter, just before Christmas, at his home, and several of us went there right from work. We car-pooled using my car and two others, leaving Lemming's car and one other one here.

"She got good and drunk," Wilson continued, "and started getting mouthy, so Smythe told me to bring her back here. I agreed and we left, with two of the others following us. But, on the way she wanted me to know what a big deal she was and she got talkative.

"She said that one day when Smythe was out of the building she went up to his office to leave some documents for him, and found that he hadn't shut down his computer before he left. She found pictures on it, pictures of the accident that killed The Wife's father."

"So, what did that mean?" McAllister asked, somewhat confused about where the conversation was heading.

The Hypocrite

"There were no pictures like that in the police file. They were taken before the police arrived, meaning Smythe either was on the scene of the 'accident,' or he knew who was driving the other car. Some of the photos showed his father-in-law before the medics got there, how he was all bloodied and busted up."

"Are you saying Smythe was involved in killing The Wife's father?" Wilson nodded. Now it was McAllister's turn to be incredulous. "So what did Lemming do?"

"She waited in the office for Smythe to come back, and when he did, she confronted him with what she had found. And she told him that he either did things her way or she would expose him to his wife, the police and the elders in the church! I think that out of all the things he faced, losing his status in the community was his biggest fear. At least that's what Lemming said."

"What made her confide all this in you?" McAllister was really curious about that aspect of what he had just been told.

"First, she was really drunk. Second, she apparently decided, due to being drunk, that she was about to have some kind of sexual encounter with me, since I was the one driving her back to the office. But what she couldn't see about herself was that she was falling asleep and then waking back up. I knew I could get out of just about any situation that arose, and I encouraged her to keep talking.

"Anyway, she was trying to impress me with what she knew and how much power she had."

"Couldn't Smythe just have deleted the files and called her bluff?"

"Maybe he could have," Wilson responded, "but he didn't know if she had made copies as she claimed. And there was more."

McAllister was literally stunned by now and just looked at Wilson as he repeated, "More?"

The Hypocrite

"Yeah," Wilson answered. "There were other pictures on Smythe's computer. Sex pictures. Lemming saw them too, and said she would tell everyone what he did when he was supposed to be working."

That part didn't impress McAllister all that much. "I don't think most people would even want to know about that, much less care," he responded to Wilson.

"Maybe not in the usual sense, I guess," Wilson said. "But these weren't your run-of-the-mill porn. These pictures were kiddy porn, children in sexual situations. That's a federal offense."

McAllister let out a long, low whistle. "So, we've been working for a freak and been manipulated by a blackmailer all this time. Terrific. So, how did this thing end with you and Lemming?"

"She was out like a light by the time we got back here so we opened the office, carried her in—which was quite the task I have to tell you—and put her on a couch that used to be in the front office. Apparently, she slept it off and went home just before dawn.

"When she saw me the next Monday she said she was glad no one came to the office before she left because her skirt was up around her waist. I have no idea about that. She wasn't in that condition when we left.

"But she thought we'd done something after we got back here, so she quit bugging me. I don't think she even remembers what she told me. I guess I should have told you, but other than quitting, I don't know what you could have done about it."

"Neither do I," McAllister answered. "Does The Wife know about this?"

"Not as far as I know," Wilson said.

McAllister thought it through for a minute, and then decided it was time to go home. But as he turned to enter the truck, the door to

The Hypocrite

Smythe Partners opened and out came the same man McAllister saw following him in Smythe's Lexus the previous week!

Without a word McAllister started walking directly toward him—Malcolm as it turned out, but McAllister didn't know his name and didn't care—stepping directly into his path on the sidewalk. Malcolm tried to avoid looking directly at McAllister and kept his eyes downcast, but McAllister wasn't giving him any consideration.

Malcolm also tried to walk around him but McAllister stepped right in front of him again, preventing any forward movement.

"Look at me, boy!" McAllister's voice was sharp and hard as steel. It was the command voice he used as a Marine NCO.

Malcolm still kept his eyes downcast, and mewled, "You're in my way."

"What are you going to do about it?" McAllister challenged. Malcolm didn't reply and McAllister put his nose less than two inches from Malcolm's, a position that would be familiar to anyone who served time as a Marine recruit and incurred the wrath of the drill instructors.

"There is a special place in Hell for cowards and traitors," McAllister said, quietly so no one else could hear him, but still with that steely hardness to his voice. "No matter what you do from now until the time you die, you can't undo your previous sins and you are destined to spend Eternity in pain and darkness. Smythe is dead, and when you die you'll be joining him in that corner of Hell."

Malcolm's face took on a look of pure terror, and he took off running for his truck. McAllister turned on his heel, a slight smile on his lips, heading back toward his truck and Wilson.

"What was that all about?" Wilson asked. "Did you know Malcolm from somewhere else?"

"Unfinished business," was all that McAllister would say.

The Hypocrite

"If they close this place down, and you need a recommendation, don't hesitate to call me," he told Wilson as he got in the truck. "You're a good guy. Don't worry about not telling me that stuff. You're right. I couldn't have done anything about it. I won't be in for the rest of the week if anyone is looking for me."

"I'm not sure any of us will be here," Wilson replied.

McAllister left the parking lot at Smythe Partners and drove straight home, taking his usual route.

Julia already knew he had survived the shooting. He had called her on his cell phone once the police cleared him and gave him a ride back to the office. She told McAllister that she saw the noon news report on the shooting, but didn't see any footage of him and didn't recognize the Rover. Initially, she had no idea he had been in any way involved.

But the police call to "next of kin," in this case The Wife, or Mrs. Smythe as the trooper referred to her, was made ahead of their final conversation with McAllister and as a result, the media was given Smythe's name before McAllister could call Julia. When he did make the call, Julia broke into tears, sobbing to him that she heard the name Smythe on the radio news and then that a second man also was dead. She called Smythe Partners but was told that McAllister was out on a client visit. Julia naturally feared the worst until he called to tell her he wasn't injured.

When McAllister pulled into the driveway, Julia flew out the front door catching him in a huge hug the second he got out of the truck. She held him tightly, as though she would never let him go, unstoppable tears coursing down her cheeks.

"I was so afraid it was you," Julia sobbed. "I couldn't get any information from anywhere. I even called the radio station, but no one knew the name of the second man. I didn't know how I could live

The Hypocrite

without you."

McAllister was not big on shows of emotion, but he held her as she let it all out. It was a bad morning for him, of that there was no doubt, but it wasn't exactly easy on her waiting at home for word on what might have happened to her husband. McAllister learned that lesson during his tours of Iraq and never took her support or her sacrifices at home lightly or for granted.

After a long while, she eased her hold on him but the tears didn't cease. They walked into the house with their arms around each other and once inside, McAllister made tea for Julia and a cup of instant decaf coffee for himself. They sat at the table sipping their drinks while he explained all that had happened earlier in the day.

The conversation went on for hours, punctuated by long silences. Finally, after making a dinner of sandwiches because neither felt like cooking or eating very much, they were exhausted and went to bed early. Julia fell into a deep sleep that was broken by nightmares. McAllister slept for an hour or two at a time but was awake for most of the night.

Julia was still working part-time and her boss was good about giving her flexible hours. On Tuesday morning she called him, explaining what had happened to her husband the previous day and asking for some time off.

"I saw the news," he said. "I figured you'd call." He readily agreed, and Julia promised to make up the missed hours later in the week.

They spent the rest of Tuesday and all day Wednesday just lounging around the house, spending time together. From time to time, Julia would ask a question as she replayed the shootout in her mind. McAllister did his best to fill in the blanks, realizing along the way that what he could see in his mind's eye was not as apparent to his wife. At one point he gave her a second-by-second replay of the morn-

The Hypocrite

ing, from the time Smythe tore out of the parking lot at the would-be client's office, until both drivers were dead.

By Wednesday afternoon, he and Julia decided that there was no more to say about the incident, and they spent the rest of that day and night watching movies. That plan was put on hold for a few hours when the doorbell rang, and upon answering it, McAllister was pleasantly surprised to find Derrick Simpson on the doorstep.

"I hope you don't mind my coming out without notice," Simpson said. "But I was really worried about you and Julia, and I just couldn't keep myself from dropping in to see how you're doing."

McAllister put on a pot of coffee, and Julia baked some mixed-berry muffins, while they all sat at the kitchen table and talked. The aroma of her baking filled the house and it was a perfect accompaniment to the brewing coffee. McAllister explained the incident to Simpson including even the smallest details, going over the actual shooting several times.

Finally, Simpson asked, "You say the police have never seen that kind of ricochet before? Meaning none of them? Not even the most experienced ones?"

"None of them ever saw anything like that, or at least that's what they told me," McAllister responded. "And they said there were myriad other factors that had to be present for that bullet to hit the shooter the way it did."

"Did they tell you what factors?" Simpson asked.

"They said the bullet first struck a steel part of the front end suspension on the Range Rover, at the perfect angle to ricochet over to the guardrail. There was a slight curve to the guardrail at that point, because of the exit ramp to I-91. That curve also came into play because that affected the path of the second ricochet.

"Then there was the temperature. It was very cold Monday

The Hypocrite

morning, and the police said the metal was less pliable than it would have been if it had been warmer, making the metal less likely to absorb the impact of the bullet and more likely to deflect it.

"And, in addition to the shooter's jerking his hand, which threw the shot off in the first place, he also was using jacketed bullets instead of hollow points. That is interesting because the hollow points will do more damage to a person and disintegrate much more easily. But the jacketed bullet stayed intact, which is what caused it to bounce off the metal in the Rover and the guardrail as well. And all of that was totally dependent on the angle of the pistol's barrel when the shot was fired."

"That is remarkable," Simpson said several times. "Did you say anything to the police about it?"

"I told them that I had either witnessed, or been in the middle of, a miracle," McAllister answered. "Or both."

"I think both," Simpson observed.

He got up to leave soon after that exchange and was at the door when he turned back to McAllister.

"I forgot to tell you. The issue with the church building was resolved yesterday!"

"Really," McAllister was hearing the first good news in several days. "What happened?"

"It seems that the federal technician was really overloaded with work and didn't realize that he made his calculations on distance to the wetlands from the nearest point of the building lot to the wetland. But the regulations say he has to make that calculation using the nearest point of the building!

"When he measured from the edge of the building instead of the edge of the lot, we gained an extra 100 feet. He apologized, signed off on the project and we can go forward in the spring. After all that has happened, he had made a simple error and we only had to bring it

The Hypocrite

to the attention of the proper people. Too bad it cost us $35,000. Or more!"

Simpson left soon after that, and McAllister and Julia settled in to watch movies. They took a break for the 6 p.m. news but went back to an action film as soon as the news was over.

The news anchorman identified the shooter, who, as it turned out, had a long and violent criminal record and was heavily involved in the drug trade. That explained his comments that he couldn't allow any witnesses, just before he tried to shoot McAllister and got himself instead.

Julia went back to work on Thursday, putting in two full days, plus a few hours on Saturday morning. By the time she signed out of work on Saturday, she had made up all the hours she missed by staying home.

They decided to resume their laid-back lifestyle for the rest of the weekend, which resulted in their taking a walk Sunday afternoon at the time when McAllister normally would have watched football. He didn't exactly give it up, however, setting his DVR to record the two games that day.

McAllister decided he would go back to work on Monday and thus would not watch the Sunday night game. When he checked the schedule and realized a good game was on at night too, he decided to throw caution to the wind and record all three games.

After returning from their walk, he dialed the code for his voice mail and retrieved the sole message. The voice on the other end was female, but she didn't identify herself. It wasn't Lemming, of that he was sure, but it could have been one of the other women from the office, or possibly The Wife.

At any rate the caller simply notified him that the office would be open at the normal time on Monday and if he wasn't coming to

The Hypocrite

work to please call and let someone know.

McAllister adhered to his usual Sunday night routine and was in bed, sound asleep by 10 p.m. The endless hours of talking through Monday's tragedy, plus the physical exertions, caught up to him all at once and he slept soundly. He was surprised to hear his alarm going off at 7 a.m., and would gladly have shut it off and slept a few more hours. But he arose, showered and got ready for work as he would on any other Monday.

He kissed Julia goodbye, left at the same time, took the same route and pulled into his usual parking spot just as he always had. But when he opened the door to Smythe Partners this day, McAllister was encountered not by Lemming, but by The Wife.

"Good morning, Bruce. I'm happy to see you today. Are you feeling better? Will you be able to work for a few hours?"

"All things considered I'm doing fine. And certainly, I'll be happy to put in a full day. But could you take a minute and fill me in on what's going on and what will be happening to the business?

The Wife took a second and then replied, "As far as the business is concerned, I have determined that the best course of action is to finish any projects that we are legally contracted to complete, and then shut the company for good. That is part of the reason I called you yesterday. I hope you don't mind being called at home.

"I also am going to give severance pay to everyone, based on length of service and the job they did here. No one will have to worry about Christmas, and I will pay you all enough to give you plenty of time to find new jobs. Most people will get a month's pay and I will also not object to their filing for unemployment.

"As far as Moran's remains are concerned, the police lab did an autopsy late Monday afternoon and released the body to me first thing Tuesday morning. He had a plot in the cemetery in Wethersfield, and

The Hypocrite

always said he wanted to be buried there, although I'm not sure why. He never lived there, and had no relatives or friends there. But he was adamant about being buried there.

"One of the parishioners works in concrete and the weather in the middle of the week was perfect so he poured a slab Tuesday for a headstone. Even though it snowed Friday, the slab was already set, so I can have a headstone placed on it any time the weather permits.

"I put his obituary in the Courant and held calling hours Wednesday night and Thursday morning, but the obit didn't run until Thursday so it was pretty much just me, some members of the parish and my family at the funeral. But his body was laid to rest in the place he wanted, and Mr. Simpson said the church will hold a graveside memorial service after Christmas, probably in early January."

McAllister took it all in, thinking to himself that The Wife just said more words in three minutes than she had since the first time he met her. He thanked her, and then turned upstairs to determine what needed to be done.

But he hesitated for a second, asking, "Where's Lemming?"

"She said she was too distraught to come to work," The Wife replied. "So I told her to take her time. I really don't need her any longer, but if she wants to put in some hours until I pull the plug I won't stop her."

McAllister walked upstairs without comment, turned on his computer and got right to work. He still had the flash drive from the week before Thanksgiving, which was a good thing because his files were tampered with again—probably the previous Monday morning while he was on the fateful trip with Smythe.

"I won't miss that crap," he thought to himself as he went through the now familiar routine of restoring his to the main computer.

There were only three companies still waiting for his services,

The Hypocrite

and McAllister attacked the tasks for each one the way he and his brother Marines attacked enemy fortifications in Iraq. He checked downstairs for coffee, was happy to find there was a full pot, freshly made, and took a half-hour break at noon to eat his lunch. The Wife was at the front desk each time, but was always occupied with other matters, and there was no further talk between them.

By 2 p.m. McAllister was finished. There was nothing else to do. He forwarded the files to the same place he always did, turned off the computer and prepared to leave. He looked around the office and realized that there was little to nothing he could call his own. He shrugged and headed down the stairs for the last time.

"Everything is done," he said to The Wife. "I put it in the file that Moran used."

"I know where it is," she replied. Then without a further word, The Wife opened the center drawer and withdrew an envelope. "This is yours, Bruce. I hope it is enough to get you through until you find another job."

McAllister took the envelope, opened it, and his eyes went as wide as saucers.

"Is it enough?" The Wife asked.

"Yes, of course," McAllister responded. "In fact it is much more than I anticipated."

"I said I would give out checks based on the work each person did and how it fit into the overall here at Smythe's. Your work was crucial to our success in many ways."

"This is three month's pay," McAllister replied, somewhat incredulous.

"I know," The Wife said. "Like I said, I hope it gets you through."

McAllister thanked her again, and then turned to go.

But he took only one step before The Wife stopped him.

The Hypocrite

"Bruce!"

He turned. "Yes?"

"You did a very good job here, and I appreciate that. Do you remember when Moran said I would be checking your work?"

To his affirmative response she said, "Well, I did. Just about every night, and quite often in the morning. You produced some excellent verbiage. I never had to make grammar or punctuation corrections, and our clients universally came back saying your facility with the language increased their sales substantially. They were all very happy with you."

"Thank you. I appreciate your saying so. I didn't get much feedback inside the office." Then it was McAllister's turn to delay his departure. "Do you mind if I ask you a question?"

"I don't mind at all," she replied.

"What's your name? Smythe just called you, The Wife, and I never heard anyone say your name in all the time I was here."

"Yvonne," she answered. "My name is Yvonne. And I can't even begin to tell you how much I loathed being called The Wife. In fact, I loathed just about everything that had anything to do with Smythe Partners. This was my father's company long before Moran Smythe showed up, and originally it was supposed to be mine after my father retired. But that never happened and things turned out much differently than any of us expected. I stayed on far longer than I should have, but I suppose the shock of my father dying and my loyalty to him combined to keep me here. I just never wanted Smythe to think he had really beat me or my father. Is there anything else you want to know?"

"A couple of things, actually," he replied. "You said you checked my files after work. Was that from home?" Yvonne nodded yes, and McAllister continued, "Did you ever notice that files here at work

The Hypocrite

were entered and manipulated after we left for the day?"

"I did, and I spoke to Moran about it numerous times, especially since it cost money to resurrect what had been destroyed. I strongly suspect Gail Lemming was behind it. In fact, I am positive she was behind it, because it happened several times when she was the only person in the office. I could tell because the computer registered each user's log-off time, and she always logged off after the files were tampered with. But Moran refused to do anything about it and took her word over mine. I could use the computer at home to access everything in this office," Yvonne said, looking directly into McAllister's eyes. "There wasn't much that could happen here in the world of Information Technology that I didn't know about."

McAllister kept his expression as neutral as was humanly possible, and was contemplating her answer when she shocked him with another question. "Bruce, did you ever see or suspect there was something going on between my husband and Gail Lemming?"

McAllister was prepared for this question long before it was asked. He knew that a lot of people suspected Smythe was more involved with Lemming than he should have been, although he doubted that anyone else knew as much as he did about that subject.

"Absolutely not," he replied with a straight face. "Besides, why on earth would any man want anything from someone like her when he was married to someone like you? That equation just doesn't add up."

Yvonne blushed, and murmured "Thank you. That was very kind."

"I call them as I see them," McAllister said. "By the way, what are you going to do now?"

"I already have a bid on the building so I'll be selling it as soon as the holidays are over and the memorial service is done. I'll put the

The Hypocrite

house on the market in the spring when prices go up. Moran had a pretty good-sized life insurance policy too, and he even named me his beneficiary, so with the money I already had, I will be fine."

"Are you going to stay in the area?"

"No," Yvonne said. "In fact I have some old college friends down in New York City who have been trying to convince me to come to work down there for a few years now. I called them, and I've been offered a job as associate editor of a national magazine they produce in Manhattan. I'm supposed to report by mid-month. So that's locked down too."

"Well, the best of luck to you," McAllister told her.

"You too," Yvonne replied. As he headed for the door she stopped him one more time. "Bruce, if you need a reference I'll give you a great one. I have your email from the personnel files and I'll contact you once I'm settled in the city. If you need a letter or a phone call, just let me know."

"Will do," McAllister said, and turned for the door one last time. "Good-bye, Yvonne."

"Good-bye, Bruce."

He walked out the door, down the sidewalk and climbed into the truck. Julia was worried sick about their finances again, but three months severance, followed by unemployment if he needed it would go a long way. He wasn't worried.

McAllister drove away one last time. He felt a sense of relief, and no regrets whatsoever. He doubted he would ever return there again. But he still had one last task for Smythe Partners on his agenda.

Chapter 14

McAllister's Revenge

Try as it might, the congregation of The Church of the Lord could not get the weather to cooperate on a suitable date for the memorial service for Moran Smythe.

Thus, it occurred that on the morning of January 23, congregants—minus Yvonne Smythe, who was already working at her new job in Manhattan—prepared themselves for a trek to the Center Cemetery in Old Wethersfield to dedicate Smythe's headstone and pay tribute to his status within their assemblage.

The date was rescheduled twice and although it didn't make the local pages of the Hartford Courant—despite Smythe's inflated opinion of himself, he never could impress the editors of the state's largest daily newspaper that he truly was a man of stature—the Rocky Hill weekly circular did dedicate a line to the service in the local happenings section. It also was in the church program the previous Sunday, leading the page four column on Parish News.

Gail Lemming, dressed in her usual less than fashionable winter garb, had stopped one last time at Smythe Partners Ltd., before at-

The Hypocrite

tending the service. The heat was on but at its lowest setting, and she shivered as she peered out the window.

She thought about what she would wear before leaving her home that morning, ultimately deciding that as unfashionable as she might appear, a pair of heavy boots and a set of earmuffs were necessary to deal with the steel-gray day and temperature hovering in the low teens. It wasn't a great day, but it was better than the weather on the days previously scheduled for the service, since there were snow storms on both of them.

The weather was due to stay cold, but there would be no precipitation, and if the service were delayed any longer, there was a good possibility that most of the parishioners would simply not attend. Lemming shrugged on her heavy overcoat, pulled on the fingerless mittens she preferred to more fashionable gloves, wrapped a long scarf around her neck, adjusted the earmuffs, and left the building looking like a refugee from some distant third-world conflict.

The heater in her car was on the fritz and not putting out anywhere near enough heat to offset the cold.

Upon entering the building earlier, using her cell phone, Lemming called a church member to bum a ride to the cemetery. Then she made a slow, tortuous journey up the stairs to Smythe's office, but it was barren. There were a lot of uncomfortable memories inside Smythe Partners and staying inside made her feel ill. She had a strong feeling of nausea and her head ached. The interior of Smythe Partners didn't look the same anyway. All the desks were gone, the computers were gone, the phone was gone, the file cabinets and the decorations were gone. Even the table where the employees ate their lunches and the elders sat at their prayer meetings was gone.

Lemming wasn't even supposed to be inside the building, but Yvonne didn't know that she still had a full set of keys to the busi-

The Hypocrite

ness. It didn't matter because the only thing that was still locked was the main door. There was just enough heat to keep the pipes from freezing and the walls from cracking. When she made her way back downstairs, she decided to wait for her ride in the parking lot. Outside would be better.

Her determination faltered within the first few minutes, however, once the cold cut through her multiple layers of outer clothing, not to mention the thick layer of body fat she carried. She was returning to the building when she heard a car horn and saw a station wagon pulling into the parking lot. Changing direction Lemming made her way to the car, squirmed into the back seat and said nearly nothing on the ride to Wethersfield.

Once in Wethersfield, however, she convinced the driver to pull in at the deli on Main Street so she could get a cup of coffee to sip during the service. Outside the car, she again was gripped by a bitter wind that shot straight down Main Street, blowing tendrils of snow before it in swirling patterns reminiscent of contrails from passing jets.

While Lemming was wrestling with the elements, McAllister was warmly ensconced in his Ford F-150, fortified and waiting for what was sure to be quite a show. About fifteen minutes earlier he had pulled into the rear parking lot of the Center Tavern, selecting a parking spot with a full view of the cemetery across the street where he enjoyed his lunches in the warmer weather. He backed into the spot to look directly at the grave site.

The grave would have been all but invisible from the street, stuck as it was far to the rear of the acreage. But it was easily observed from McAllister's vantage point thanks to the plastic flowers that surrounded it and the wind-whipped tarp over the speaker's platform, both placed there the previous afternoon by parishioners.

Before parking in the tavern lot, a full half-hour before the

The Hypocrite

scheduled start of the service, McAllister had made one other stop, at the deli nearby on Main Street, the same one where Lemming was now brusquely ordering coffee. Rather than coffee, however, McAllister bought a steaming mug of hot chocolate.

He had pulled into the parking space near the building and as customers preceded him into the small shop, he noted the sharp report of high heels on the cement sidewalks, so cold and hard that they absorbed nearly no noise at all. The street-facing windows were steamed, and inside the staff hustled as they moved orders of breakfast sandwiches and warm drinks.

"I'll miss this," McAllister thought to himself. Of all that had occurred in the previous year only this deli—next to the barbershop advertising discount rates for the half-bald and elderly—stood out positively in his mind. He regretted that he never followed through on a mental promise to stick his head into the barber shop and find out from the owner exactly at which point of hair loss a customer was considered "bald." The answer would have to remain one of life's great mysteries.

Inside the deli, the staff greeted him by name and offered him a fresh baked oatmeal and apple cookie to accompany his drink, an offer he gladly accepted. The food here was fantastic, creative and ample, and he was accepted as a regular within weeks of making his first luncheon visit.

McAllister paid for his order, said "goodbye" as opposed to his customary "see you later" and walked back to the curb. No one noticed the language change, and even if they did, he had no intention of discussing why he wouldn't be coming this way again.

In the tavern parking lot, he sipped at the chocolate, burned his lip, then put it on the dashboard to cool. The cookie was fresh but McAllister decided he could wait to eat it so the complementary fla-

The Hypocrite

vors of oatmeal and apple could accompany the dark sweetness of the drink.

Cars passed, even a local police cruiser, but no one so much as glanced his way, much less paid attention to his vehicle. He kept the engine running and the heater on, pushing a Rolling Stones Greatest Hits CD into the player for entertainment.

Within fifteen minutes, a small line of cars, mostly American-made family sedans and station wagons—as opposed to the more expensive vehicles favored by Smythe—pulled into the cemetery and parked as close to the grave as the road allowed, leaving about fifty feet to walk through the snow. The group exited the vehicles and stood huddled against the wind. Everyone was bundled in a similar fashion—scarves, long coats, boots and gloves for the women—overcoats, hats and gloves for the men.

All the clothing was a somber gray or black, right down to their boots. There was a moment of milling around, until Simpson took the lead and headed toward the grave. No one seemed to notice a line of black arrows in the snow pointing toward the headstone, or if they did, it didn't register as odd or unusual, and the pack of boot-clad feet soon obliterated the tracks near the arrows.

Simpson strode confidently toward the grave, the shivering congregation, numbering about a dozen, now strung out behind him. It was hardly the massive crowd that Smythe envisioned in his reveries. In fact, it was a comparatively tiny gathering, and not at all in keeping with Smythe's vision of his death as the catalyst for a great regional outpouring of grief.

From his vantage point McAllister couldn't help chuckling at the small turnout. "If I could see inside those heads," he mused, "I bet I'd find more than half of them are here just to make sure the miserable S.O.B. is really dead."

The Hypocrite

Simpson was within the length of a tall man's body from the speaker's stand when he suddenly halted, stopping as though he had hit a wall. Those nearest him bumped into his back, others hitting them like dominoes that start to fall but never quite have the energy to finish the movement.

The mourners nearest the grave suddenly gasped, nearly in unison as they realized why Simpson stopped so abruptly. No one in the front of the group moved for a long minute, until Lemming, who was bringing up the rear, created a small commotion by pushing her way to the front.

"What is it? What's going on? Why did everyone stop? Let ... me ... *through!*"

She shoved and maneuvered her way to the front, encountering cold stares from the congregation as she passed. The looks weren't lost on Lemming, and she decided that as soon as this little charade was over, she would deal with those who suddenly turned unfriendly. She was used to the deference that she believed was her due as Smythe's right hand, and even though he was gone, she assumed it would continue.

She was wrong.

Finally, breaching the solid wall of men's shoulders that formed a barrier to the grave, she approached Simpson with her customary brusqueness. "Why are you just standing there? Let's get moving on this, everyone is freezing! Do you hear me? Are you even listening to me?"

Quickly running out of breath, Lemming finally realized that neither Simpson nor any of the elders who flanked him were paying even scant attention to her. Their eyes were fixed on the ground in front of the headstone. She followed Simpson's gaze, then, like the others in front who had been the first to view the scene, gasped and

The Hypocrite

stood rigidly quiet.

A message was left on the ground in front of the headstone, a message for Smythe and all who were weak enough to follow or support him.

The message said simply, Matt. 7:17. It was a bright, bright orange color that stood out like neon against the white snow.

"What the hell is that supposed to mean?" Lemming snarled to no one in particular.

Simpson looked at her with hard eyes. "Matthew chapter seven, verse seventeen, it looks like to me," he said. "Most real Christians would at least have a minimal understanding of the form and the section of the Bible it's from."

"Well, what does Matthew seven, seventeen say?" This time Lemming's tone was snide, as if Simpson should beg her forgiveness and plead with her to let him continue.

"It related to people who profess to be messengers of the Lord, but in truth are false prophets," Simpson said. "It makes the very clear point that God doesn't like people claiming to speak for Him when He didn't ask them to, or give them permission.

"I believe it says, *Even so every good tree bringeth forth good fruit; but a corrupt tree bringeth forth evil fruit.* An appropriate message for our dearly departed former treasurer, wouldn't you agree? Didn't he claim to be the descendant of the founders of Wethersfield?" Simpson continued, with a voice as cold and hard as the sidewalks a block away. "Didn't he claim they were upstanding Christians who followed the word of God? Wasn't all that just a huge lie?"

As the impact of Simpson's words set in, Lemming felt a sudden force hit her chest, as though she was struck in the sternum by a doubled-up fist. The first shock wave was barely subsiding when she felt another, this one accompanied by an overwhelming sense of fatigue.

The Hypocrite

She tried to speak to Simpson but no words came. Her vision became blurry, then everything quickly went dark and she lost all sensation. Transfixed as they were by the message on the ground, no one noticed Lemming's discomfort until she suddenly collapsed in a heap at their feet.

"Oh, my God! What's happening?" a woman queried, but no one answered.

Rather than stepping in to help, the congregation stepped back from Lemming as one, seemingly cued by an invisible hand. Her face by now was a mottled purple and what appeared to be attempts to speak came out only as "Aarrrgggh, aarrrgggh!"

Lemming's arms flailed about her and her feet kicked into the air, pushing her skirt up past her knees, exposing grossly oversized thighs padded with huge clumps of cellulite, looking like a bad batch of unfinished cottage cheese. Foam began oozing from her mouth, and still no one moved.

An elder touched Simpson's forearm, asking "Shouldn't we do something for her?"

Simpson nodded and immediately knelt beside Lemming, beginning a rapid double-hand pumping directly on her sternum. A woman in the crowd asked if there wasn't something more that should be done.

"Do you want to give her mouth-to-mouth?" Simpson replied, referring to her still foaming maw. "Besides," he added, "I don't have a certificate in first aid and I wouldn't want to do something wrong. People get sued these days for misdirected medical attention."

The congregation took all this in without comment, mulling over Simpson's warning. "Still," a member finally ventured, "we should at least call for an ambulance. I wouldn't want to see the church held liable."

The Hypocrite

"Agreed," Simpson answered, forcing his eyes back to the spectacle on the ground. Then, "Does anyone have a cell phone?"

A half-dozen phones appeared and Simpson nodded to the holder of the one nearest to him. He returned to his ministrations not really seeing the man dialing first for information, then the number of the local fire department for routine calls, rather than 911. Another minute elapsed before he finally was connected to the dispatcher at fire headquarters and reported a medical emergency at Center Cemetery.

"What's the nature of the emergency?"

"It appears to be a fainting spell."

"What is the description of the victim?"

"Caucasian woman, late forties, very, very heavy."

"Does the victim have any allergies to drugs?"

"I wouldn't know."

"Do you have a reading on her pulse?"

"No."

"Is she breathing?"

"She appears to be."

"Okay, the ambulance is on the way. It will be there in just a few minutes. Please stay on the line, and if you can have someone monitor her vital signs it would be helpful."

"Fine, I'll do that."

While Simpson was continuing his efforts at CPR, the dispatcher signaled for the ambulance crew and EMT, who normally waited in the crew's lounge next to the communication center. It was only a few steps to the garage housing the ambulance, and the driver leaped into the cab, only to find that the EMT was missing.

Quickly leaping out again, he ran to the men's room, throwing open the door and noting that one stall was closed. A pair of work

The Hypocrite

boots was visible below the stall door.

"Medical emergency, let's roll," the driver called.

"What kind of emergency?" came from inside the booth.

"Fainting spell in the Center Cemetery, let's get moving."

"Be right there."

It was another full minute before the ambulance pulled out of the garage, engaged its siren and headed for the cemetery. By then Lemming had stopped moving and breathing. Simpson half-heartedly asked if anyone knew how to monitor vital signs, but no one responded.

Her thrashing arms and feet had made impressions in the snow that from another, smaller person could have resembled snow angels.

But her fingerless mittens and her boots combined to give her extremities the appearance of hooves, and the depression where her head flopped to and fro was punctuated by the earmuffs with sharp upward pointing marks that some later would remark looked strangely like horns.

While the ambulance was on its quick voyage to the cemetery, Lemming's face took on a grayish hue. By now she had breathed her last, and her death mask was permanently fixed in a vile combination of rage and unspeakable fear.

Simpson finally stopped his efforts at CPR and began staring off into space as though his mind was anywhere but on the ground before him. Finally, Simpson stood, saying nothing for a moment as he stared transfixed at Lemming and the impression she had left in the snow. He was snapped back to the present by a tug on his sleeve from Elder Anderson, who was standing next to him.

"What do you think she saw at the last moment ... to have her face end up like that, I mean?"

"I don't know," Simpson replied, "but whatever it was, I hope we never see the same thing." He shivered involuntarily.

The Hypocrite

The ambulance pulled into the cemetery, and the crowd parted so the crew could get to Lemming. The EMT checked her pulse, checked for breathing, and after a moment looked up at the mourners.

"I'm sorry," he said, to no one in particular. "She's gone. Looks like a heart attack. There was nothing anyone could do."

As one, the parishioners turned away and started back to their cars, the memorial service forgotten.

From his vantage point across the street McAllister watched the drama unfold in complete shock. The cookie and hot chocolate were long gone, and he had thought he would be witnessing a comedy of sorts.

He intended to make his point about Smythe nearly getting him killed, and in a larger sense, about the way Smythe treated those around him while professing to spread the word of Jesus. If Lemming got the message, so much the better.

But he never intended any further harm to anyone. Enough harm already was done and once today's service was over, it was McAllister's intent to put it all behind him and devote all his energy to finding a new job.

But as the crew fit Lemming into a body bag, McAllister felt conflicting emotions that ranged from pity to a strange sense of satisfaction that things turned out even better than he had hoped. "I'll probably have to answer for this someday," he mused.

The message on the ground in front of Smythe's headstone was his, of course, and it was the last piece of writing he would ever do for Smythe Partners, Ltd. McAllister had taken three days to prepare for it.

First, he cut back on his intake of fluids, while simultaneously upping his cardio workouts to an hour and swallowing 10,000 CCs of Vitamin C each day. Starting at 8 p.m. on the night before the memorial service McAllister drank two sixteen ounce beers, then two quarts

The Hypocrite

of water while he sat in his great room watching the news. When he finished he told Julia he needed to make a quick run to the store and would be back shortly.

Then he made the ride to Wethersfield, and parked behind the Center Tavern exactly as he did this morning. Several cars were still in the parking lot, but no one was outside, the patrons preferring instead to nurse their dinners and avoid the bitter cold for as long as possible.

McAllister slipped across the street unseen, and headed for Smythe's grave, putting down the black arrows every twenty feet or so. He didn't want anyone to miss the grave the next day.

When he reached the headstone, McAllister stood in front of it, perhaps five feet from the base, and straddled the grave, his feet wider apart than the width of his shoulders. He unzipped his fly and let loose with three-quarters of a gallon of fluids that had been building in his bladder.

The stream hit the snow in short precisely aimed bursts, and, due to the buildup of impurities and Vitamin C in his system, was a dark shade of yellow, nearly orange, that stood in stark contrast to the white snow.

When he finished, he backed away carefully, returned to the truck, washed his hands with pre-moistened wipes, and drove to Route 3, and ultimately home. He went to the great room, and resumed his position in his chair, prompting Julia to remark that he hadn't brought anything home from the store.

"They were closed," he said, and returned to the news.

The grave remained undisturbed overnight, and the message that greeted the congregation as they arrived for the service was as McAllister had left it—frozen in place until the next thaw or the next snowstorm came to cover it. No one thought, or cared, to erase it and as the ambulance crew was about to load Lemming's body into the

The Hypocrite

back for the ride to the morgue, the EMT noticed the bright marking.

"Who would have done that?" he asked the driver as they examined the handwork. "And what does it mean?"

"Search me," the driver said, gesturing at the headstone. He looked closely at the inscription and remarked to the EMT that he once had dealings with Smythe that were not pleasant. "Knowing him, it could have been anybody—and it probably wasn't good." They both broke out in laughter as they departed without disturbing the site further, and the message was left for all to see.

When the ambulance left the cemetery, McAllister pulled out of the tavern parking lot and retraced his ride home from the night before. By the time he reached Route 2 on the far side of the Connecticut River, the Stones were singing Gimme Shelter, and he joined in the chorus, "It's just a shot away, just a shot away" in full voice.

Not a bad piece of work, McAllister mused as he drove. The message was clear, and got the point across with as few words as possible. The location was just right for the target audience to encounter it, the choice of color and background made sure it would be noticed. It was an ad man's dream, a marketing model in real life.

McAllister sincerely believed it represented his best effort for Smythe Partners, Ltd.

Benediction

When McAllister left the cemetery and drove up the entrance ramp to I-91, he quickly entered the highway, then took the second exit to state Route 3, which connected to state Route 2 on the other side of the Connecticut River.

On a normal day he would only need a few miles worth of exits before he got off in semi-rural, semi-suburban greater Hartford, in what once was a farming community but now was considered a "bedroom" town.

But when he reached his exit, McAllister kept going south on Route 2, not exactly sure why. He drove nearly to Norwich, but, before reaching the end of the limited access highway, took the exit for I-395 south, reaching the exit that led directly to the Mohegan Sun casino in a matter of minutes. He was there when it first opened, when it was smaller and rustic. Now it was huge, the inevitable result of the billions of dollars poured into the gaming tables and slot machines over the past decades.

McAllister wasn't even sure why he was here, and why he chose

The Hypocrite

the Sun over Foxwoods. He could have reached that casino with only a few more minutes of driving, but for some reason he didn't feel like driving through Norwich, even though years of traveling to the Rhode Island beaches taught him a shortcut that bypassed much of the summer traffic and in the winter was all but deserted.

At any rate, he parked, and entered the gambling hall. He wandered for a few minutes, then located the blackjack tables with five-dollar minimum bets. He found a seat, pulled five, twenty-dollar bills from his wallet and exchanged them for chips. He played conservatively for the next hour or so, at times hitting a decent bet, at others losing a few dollars. He never was down more than twenty dollars and never up more than that amount either. Pretty girls in Indian costumes came by occasionally, asking if he wanted a drink, but he declined each time.

Players making much bigger bets were seated on each side, and he vaguely noted that they were dropping large sums fairly regularly. After nearly an hour, McAllister gave himself another fifteen minutes of playing time, and this time accepted a drink of whiskey and ginger when he was asked. He hit a couple of times, then lost once, then hit again. The drink disappeared quickly and he ordered another.

He placed one final bet, hit again, then asked the dealer, a youngish man-boy with a pock-marked face and bored, nearly hostile demeanor, to cash him out.

"Should I call security to help with your winnings, sir?" the dealer asked sarcastically as he handed over the cash. McAllister paused to count the money, making a show of it just to spite the little punk.

"No," he finally answered. "I do appreciate the offer though. Let's see. I just played my favorite card game for an hour, had drinks on the house, and as I see it, made a fifty-dollar profit. Not a bad haul.

The Hypocrite

I should do this more often."

The dealer feigned indifference and went on with the game. The high rollers both chuckled, then both went bust with hundred-dollar bets on the table. McAllister walked away chuckling to himself.

When asked later on, he couldn't recall why he did what he did next. Perhaps it was a remembrance of his father telling him about casinos, how you stood the best chance on the slots if you played a machine on the end of an aisle near a heavily traveled walkway, preferably one where someone else was playing, but not winning, for an hour or more.

As he passed the ten-dollar slots, McAllister saw an elderly man get up from his stool at an end machine and walk away disgustedly.

Without a thought McAllister slipped onto the stool and slipped five twenty-dollar bills into the slot, noted that the machine registered his credit, and pulled the handle—he preferred the old one-armed style to pushing the PLAY button. Somehow that button just seemed too far removed from any semblance of control.

The old man he had replaced ambled by on the way toward the exit and told McAllister, "Good luck, I've been on that damned machine all day and got nothing." McAllister nodded, but said nothing, and pulled the lever again. There was nothing dramatic about what happened next, no forewarning, no premonition. He hit a couple of small jackpots, lost on a couple more turns then watched almost disinterestedly on the sixth attempt as three cherries lined up perfectly.

He was still taking it in as the bells and whistles started, lights began flashing and out of nowhere casino security surrounded him. The "ding, ding, ding" of a winning machine was sounding, and sounding, and sounding. People began slapping McAllister on the back and offering him drinks.

"What is it?" he asked the nearest security agent, a hard-bod-

The Hypocrite

ied, thirty-something blond who Julia would have called a hunk.

"What is it?" came the incredulous reply. "Man, you hit the big one, a million!"

What came next was pretty much contained in a mélange of noise and colors that McAllister was sure he would carry with him the rest of his days. He was ushered to the casino main office, people took pictures of him, and an IRS agent showed up almost immediately, but was offset by a complimentary accountant supplied by Mohegan Sun.

The accountant explained that McAllister would have to pay taxes on the winnings before he left the premises, but also gave him some excellent advice on spreading out the payments and making more in the long run. When McAllister finally left, it was with a check for more than $100,000, a binding contract from the casino explaining how the remainder would be paid, and the names of several lawyers and accountants who could help him deal with the windfall.

McAllister drove to the nearest branch of his bank to make a deposit, then drove the rest of the way home on air, pulling into the driveway, parking and walking slowly inside like a man in a dream.

"Hi, Hon," Julia greeted him. "Is everything okay?"

McAllister nodded without speaking.

"Where have you been?" she asked. "I was getting a little worried."

McAllister went to the kitchen without answering, opened his wife's pocketbook and removed her checkbook. He took a pen from the junk drawer under the countertop, and sat down at the table to write.

Julia walked into the room with a bewildered look on her face, and asked again. "Is everything okay?"

The Hypocrite

Again McAllister said nothing, but this time handed her a check made out to CASH for $10,000.

"Have yourself some fun," he said. "There's more where that came from." Then and only then, did he begin to relate the events of his day.

Afterward, McAllister told Julia, "I'll grill us some steaks if you go get them. And on the way back, could you grab a bottle of scotch and a cigar for me?"

Julia grabbed the keys and was halfway out the door before stopping to ask what kind of scotch he wanted. She already knew where to get him a cigar. The scotch was a different matter.

"Glenmorangie," he said. "Nectar D'Or. They have it down the hill."

Julia ran the errands, bringing back two twelve ounce porterhouse steaks. He took them outside on a platter along with a set of tongs. The grill cover was already removed and McAllister opened the supply valve to the propane gas tank. He had brought the cooking grid inside and washed it off in the sink while Julia was at the store, so the grill was prepared by the time she returned, and he quickly lit the fire.

He set it on high and then McAllister went right to work grilling the steaks, while Julia made a salad. She had picked up a fresh loaf of Italian bread at the store to go with the dinner, and had purchased a California White Zinfandel to go with her meal.

He brought the steaks inside when they were done and set them on the table to rest a few minutes before they started eating. The food was delicious, but neither one spoke much, both lost in their thoughts, plans, and the laborious process of absorbing all that had occurred in the past few hours.

Under normal circumstances McAllister would eat the New

The Hypocrite

York Strip portion of the Porterhouse, leaving the cut on the other side of the T-bone for a breakfast of steak and eggs the next morning. But he was so absorbed in his thoughts that he just kept cutting and eating, occasionally stopping to dip a piece of bread into the juices.

"Is your steak good?" Julia asked, more to make conversation than anything else.

"It's perfect," McAllister replied, and it was. He had grilled his to a perfect medium and Julia's to medium-well.

At one point, a slight smile curled the corners of his mouth. But he declined to tell Julia that his thoughts centered on how she was probably thinking of ways to spend the money—while he was figuring how to save it. They'd deal with that later, he decided wisely.

Afterward, she collected the dishes and McAllister walked out onto the deck overlooking the backyard. It was cold, but not frigid, and after the warmth of the kitchen the bite of a January night in New England was refreshing. It was late now, the sky in the west long since fading from the bright orange-red of sunset to a dark purple. Overhead the stars were shining with a stark whiteness against the black sky.

He had opened the scotch after dinner, splashing two fingers of the amber fluid over three ice cubes in a tumbler, and carrying it out on the deck along with his cigar, cutter and lighter. He lit his cigar—an Ashton Corona—and puffed on it, not inhaling, but blowing the smoke out of his mouth in a long stream. McAllister rarely smoked, and when he did it was never cigarettes. But he did enjoy a celebratory cigar once or twice a year, especially a high-end quality cigar such as an Ashton or an Avo. This was one of those times.

In all that had occurred in the previous months, there was one facet of McAllister's existence that was completely unknown by his tormentors, focused as they were on their own egos and points

The Hypocrite

of view. He told Smythe at his initial interview that he was raised a Methodist, and went to church and Sunday School nearly every week as a youth. But that was pretty much the extent of what Smythe knew about him, and in fact, Smythe was so self-centered that he really didn't care about McAllister's background.

But there was a lot more to McAllister's religious upbringing. In his teens he attended retreats with other Methodist youth, and studied the Bible extensively before and during his confirmation process. He still remembered his grandmother starting each day on the farm by putting on the coffee for his grandfather, and then reading a daily verse from her well-worn Bible.

He experienced moments of doubt as an adult, especially after seeing the horrors of war, but his doubts always centered on the way some humans exploited others who had similar doubts but couldn't work them out alone. He never stopped believing there was far more in the universe than mere mortals could know at this stage in their development, and that much of what existed was far more powerful and far more important than he was.

Those thoughts were running through his mind as McAllister enjoyed the smoke and the scotch. He sipped from his drink, letting the whisky rest at the roof of his mouth, savoring its slightly smoky flavor before letting it slide over the back of his tongue and down his throat, hitting his stomach with a welcome fire.

"Well, you sure surprised me on this one," he said to no one in particular, although he was looking skyward when he spoke. "I know I haven't exactly been the best of messengers over the years, but I think even you'll have to admit that the message can be very confusing. It gets lost sometimes too, and it takes a while to find it again. It's kind of like losing your keys or your glasses. You know you had them, you just can't remember where you left them."

The Hypocrite

He continued, talking to no one in particular, but certain that somehow, someway his words were not the idle chatter of a mind that was just releasing the stress of the past months, or even the past decade.

"Let's see if I have this all in order. First, I witness an attack on our country that is unprecedented going back to the War of 1812. As a result the economy collapses, my business suffers and I enlist in the Marines to take the battle to the people who attacked us. I fight in a war, then come home to a country that is in a state of chaos, get so far behind in my bills that I have to take the first job that comes along, working for a guy who claims to have an inside track with the Almighty—that would be You—but in reality is a hypocrite and bully.

"Then of all the people he deals with in his daily life, it is up to me to be the one who challenges him, even if I never say a word, even if it is with just my presence, my very existence if you will. And, of course, You will.

"I even become a focal point in the internal affairs of his church, even though I don't belong to his church, and that ticks him off so much that he tries to take it out on other drivers on the highway, which gets him shot, and nearly gets me shot, too. And now he is dead, his mistress is dead, a violent felon is dead in the process, and suddenly financially I am set for life."

McAllister paused for a moment, letting it all sink in. Then he continued, "I bet some people would say this is all just a bunch of random occurrences.

"And I realize that when one comes right down to it, that as much of a hypocrite as Smythe was, I can be and have been as much a hypocrite as anyone else, I guess. But you have to admit, at least my heart is in the right place and always has been."

McAllister suddenly chuckled to himself, "You know, if Julia

The Hypocrite

comes out here and finds me talking to myself, she just might have me committed and keep all the money for herself."

He went silent then, and for the first time in a very, very long time McAllister enjoyed a sensation of true peace. He knew that he did not have the answers to the myriad questions that plagued him and have probably plagued others for the entirety of human existence. He also knew that it was doubtful he would find those answers in his lifetime.

But, he also reflected, what would humans do if they knew everything there was to know? Perhaps it was a required facet of humanity to always have questions, to always have a quest, a thirst for knowledge, a need to know. Perhaps that was the ultimate answer—that there would always be questions.

McAllister could see the glow from the lights of Hartford to the west offsetting the dark of the night. Their reflection on the few clouds in the sky gave the night a welcome luminance. It was very still, no breeze at all, and cold, but he felt comfortable.

To his right he could see the branches of the huge sugar maple that bordered the lawn. It was his favorite tree, and while it reflected a stark beauty now, only a couple of months earlier it was emblazoned with a bright red blanket of leaves as summer turned to fall. In a few months the leaves again would appear, filling in heavily and providing welcome shade when it was needed. It was a reassuring thought.

Suddenly, a slight wind brushed back his hair, and although the night air was cold, the breeze felt warm as though he had been touched by a gentle hand. Then, as the warm glow of the scotch spread throughout his midsection, McAllister paused, looked upward again for a moment, generally in the direction of Orion, raised his glass and whispered "Thank You."

And in the furthest, most distant reaches of the universe, far be-

The Hypocrite

yond the swirling galaxies, secure from the noiseless black holes, insulated by dark matter that had no purpose other than to confuse mere mortals who had the audacity to think they had it all figured out, the Almighty stopped, ever so briefly, and smiled, ever so slightly, before returning to the task of long-range planning.

About the Author

Ron Winter is an author, public relations executive, and award winning journalist. He has written two non-fiction books, Masters of the Art, A Fighting Marine's Memoir of Vietnam published by Random House, and *Granny Snatching, How a 92-Year-Old Widow Fought the Courts and Her Family to Win Her Freedom,* published by Nightengale Press.

Ron's latest book, *The Hypocrite,* also published by Nightengale Press, is his first novel.

Ron flew 300 combat missions as a Marine helicopter machine gunner in Vietnam and was awarded 15 Air Medals, Combat Aircrew Wings, and the Vietnamese Cross of Gallantry among many other decorations.

After Vietnam he earned undergraduate degrees in Electrical Engineering and English Literature. In a two-decade journalism career Ron was the recipient of several prestigious awards for public service and a Pulitzer nomination.

He is married and has three children.

www.ingramcontent.com/pod-product-compliance
Lightning Source LLC
Chambersburg PA
CBHW071337080526
44587CB00017B/2874